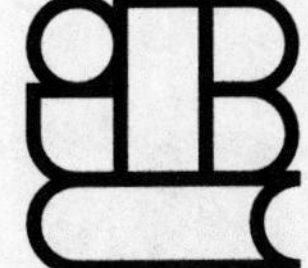

The Corporate Culture Survival Guide

Edgar H. Schein

Foreword by Warren Bennis

The Corporate Culture Survival Guide

Sense and Nonsense About Culture Change

Jossey-Bass Publishers • San Francisco

Jossey-Bass books and products are available through most bookstores. To contact Jossey-Bass directly, call (888) 378-2537, fax to (800) 605-2665, or visit our website at www.josseybass.com.

Substantial discounts on bulk quantities of Jossey-Bass books are available to corporations, professional associations, and other organizations. For details and discount information, contact the special sales department at Jossey-Bass.

Manufactured in the United States of America on Lyons Falls Turin Book. This paper is acid-free and 100 percent totally chlorine-free.

Library of Congress Cataloging-in-Publication Data

Schein, Edgar H.
The corporate culture survival guide: sense and nonsense about culture change / Edgar H. Schein; foreword by Warren Bennis. — 1st ed.
p. cm.
"A Warren Bennis book."
Includes bibliographical references and index.
ISBN 0-7879-4699-0 (acid-free paper)
1. Corporate culture. 2. Culture. 3. Organizational behavior. I. Title.
HD58.7 .S3217 1999
65.4'06—dc21

99-6330

first edition
HB Printing 10 9 8 7 6 5 4 3 2 1

Warren Bennis

A Warren Bennis Book

This collection of books is devoted exclusively to new and exemplary contributions to management thought and practice. The books in this series are addressed to thoughtful leaders, executives, and managers of all organizations who are struggling with and committed to responsible change. My hope and goal is to spark new intellectual capital by sharing ideas positioned at an angle to conventional thought—in short, to publish books that disturb the present in the service of a better future.

Other Books in the Warren Bennis Signature Series

Self-Esteem at Work by Nathaniel Branden
A *Spiritual Audit of Corporate America* by Ian I. Mitroff and Elizabeth A. Denton

Contents

Foreword

Ed Schein knows a thing or two about corporate culture. Ed Schein also knows a thing or two about organizational change. The truth is that Ed Schein probably knows more about corporate culture and its relevance for organizational transformation than just about anybody writing about these issues today. If there is such a thing as "principled envy," then this is the book that a good many of us would have wished we had written. Let me tell you why.

First of all, Schein has been at it a long, long time, some forty years or so, both on the ground, consulting with dozens of organizations, and then drawing on those experiences plus some thorough empirical research to create, if you will, a theory of practice of cultural transformation. I have come across many in this field who have written about corporate culture without ever taking part in the sweaty, gritty, and complex job of guiding institutions to a new state. What they've done is read up on it, so to speak. And then I have come across the practitioners who are mainly concerned with producing events and acting without the 30,000-foot view or having the time or opportunity to reflect on these matters. The first are always inclined to think abstractly, to find over-arching principles, while the latter, living in a world disconnected from facts, are often prone to imagine that everything can be explained or attributable to particular incidents. We can call one "participative truth" and the other "observed truth." Both, for obvious reasons, are limited and each of them can be equally deceived. Each should be capable of informing the other. Which is exactly what Schein does. He has the unique capacity to blend these two kinds of truth in what can be called "practical intelligence": knowledge of use to the practicing manager and consultant but also of use to the academic with that 30,000-foot perspective.

Secondly, Schein writes with unbridled lucidity. In fact, his clarity is what gives this volume real power. In the service of full disclosure, I should tell you that Ed and I have worked together for many years and coauthored two books. No one I have worked with has quite the knack he does for taking complex ideas and rendering them in such simple, clear declarative sentences. His writing is spare and muscular, and when he uses charts and diagrams to illustrate a point, they do just that: they clarify and illuminate. But not for a moment is this book simplistic nor does it try to vulgarize by oversimplifying the subtle nuances of culture. Oliver Wendell Holmes put it best (and I'm paraphrasing him) when he said, "I wouldn't give a fig for the simplicity this side of or before complexity but I would gladly lay down my life for the simplicity on the other side of complexity." That's the gift of this book, rendering simplicity on the other side of complexity.

Finally, what makes this book so wonderful is that it takes culture seriously. That sounds weird, doesn't it? Why wouldn't a book on corporate culture be serious? Schein argues, and he's spot on, that there's too much palaver written about corporate culture; you know the six easy steps to change the world. He avoids quick fixes, catchy phrases, simplistic bromides, and fervent anthems. In fact, he regularly reminds us that culture is something that is delicate and tough, adamantine in nature, not difficult to misread and hazardous when you do. The subtext of this terrific book is that you just can't pop a culture in microwave and out pops a McCulture.

Schein's book is the distillation of forty years of reflection and research, experience and imagination. What a treat to read, principled envy and all.

June 1999

Warren Bennis
University Professor
Marshall School of Business
University of Southern California

Preface

I have always advised my students to write when they feel passionate about something. Some of my own best writing over the years has been precipitated by anger—something that seemed clear to me was so unclear to others. So I sat down to try to clarify it as best I could. This feeling has overcome me again with respect to organizational culture.

The concept of culture was introduced by anthropologists more than one hundred years ago, and anyone who travels or takes an anthropology course feels personally how differently different people think and do things. The traveler also learns that it is dangerous to stereotype another culture. It is easy and convenient, but it is dangerous, especially when there are superficial similarities, if getting things done in the other culture matters. If I want to work in Germany, it does me little good to know that Germans are compulsive; if I want to work in Italy, it is not so helpful to know that Italians are free in expressing their emotions; and if a German wants to work in the United States, it is of little good to know that we are individualistic. These insights can be helpful, but they are not enough. Cultures are *patterns* of interacting elements; if we don't have a way of deciphering the patterns then we may not understand the cultures at all.

Now, here is my puzzle and frustration. Why do we assume that organizations—corporations with long and venerable histories, or even young companies with short but intensive histories—are simpler to decipher than countries? All of our case evidence suggests that these organizations develop powerful cultures that guide the thinking and behavior of their employees. Yet we talk about corporate culture as if it were a managerial tool, like a new form of organization structure. Every day, the papers are full of managers announcing that they need a "new culture" of something or other in their organization, and there are plenty of consultants ready to come in and give them a program for launching their new culture. Can you imagine saying that the United States, or France, needs a new culture?

To make matters worse, we know that managers like things that are quantifiable, measurable, and manipulable. Management is being in control of something, not drifting along with the tide. Managers favor concepts and tools that are actionable. So, unfortunately, many academics and consultants tout culture concepts and theories based on questionnaires that produce numbers and profiles, and that permit organizations to be put into neat boxes. But when I visit those organizations, what I observe is that the boxes contain only some of the superficial elements of the culture. They are not incorrect labels, but they are fairly useless because they do not reflect the cultural forces that matter. In my experience, the forces that matter cannot be dug out with simple measures; they cannot easily be classified into typologies because they tend to be unique patterns reflecting the unique history of the organization.

So I am writing again, to supplement my longer books of 1985 and 1992 (*Organizational Culture and Leadership*, first and second editions respectively), and to be more pointed in my argument. There is now abundant evidence that corporate culture makes a difference to corporate performance; we know that leaders increasingly need concepts and tools for working with culture in varied and subtle ways. If you want to take a serious rather than superficial look at culture in organizations, struggle through this book with me—and let the complexity inform you rather than turn you off. You will not find Three Steps to the Perfect Corporate Culture. But you may gain some insights and ideas to help you deal more constructively with the culture issues you have in your organization.

In each chapter, I provide the logic of the argument, but I also give you case material and practical suggestions for what you can do to test the ideas for yourself. I hope the chapter titles are self-explanatory; you should feel free to jump around to follow your own questions. I find that learning to see the world through culturally more sophisticated lenses is fun. You see more, and you understand more. I hope that you too discover that it is fun to have cultural insight.

Methodology and Acknowledgments

I have learned over the past forty years that the best data about what goes on in the real world come from real-world experience. I have learned the most about organizations and their cultures from actual experiences as a member of and consultant to organizations. Consulting to organizations proves to be critical because until someone seeks help and until the consultant tries to provide help, much of the reality of what is going on remains hidden. The traditional researcher cannot motivate the members of an organization to reveal what they spend a lot of energy concealing, and in fact much of what the researcher wants to know is even hidden by the organization's members from themselves.

It is when the organization wants something, when it seeks help, that the psychological dynamic is set up for finding out what is really going on. Kurt Lewin had it right when he said that you cannot understand an organization until you try to change it. I found that when I functioned as a helper or consultant, I could observe things and ask about things that revealed the underbelly of organizational life where cultural issues reside. I called this "clinical research" (Schein, 1987) and have argued that this level of inquiry is necessary and desirable for deciphering cultural issues (Schein, 1993). The clinical researcher brings theory and helping skills to client systems that want to solve problems and discovers during his or her interaction with the clients that all sorts of important data surface about what is going on. Documenting, organizing, and extrapolating from these data is the essence of clinical research, and it is what most of my cultural knowledge is based on.

Because most of what I have learned comes from my consulting work with organizations, it is to those organizations that I owe a major debt of gratitude. It is the willingness of organizations to let me help them, hang around, ask questions, give lectures and get responses, and run workshops and simulations in which I could observe people in action that has nurtured my own insight into cultural and organizational dynamics. I wish to thank all of my clients, particularly Digital Equipment, Ciba-Geigy, "Alpha" Power, "Beta" Oil, and the dozens of others who have let me see a bit of their cultural reality.

The insights I have gained from my clinical experience in working with organizations combined with what I know of theory and what other researchers have uncovered is the basis for the assertions made in this book. We are not yet, in this field, at the stage of having hard hypotheses to test, and perhaps we never will be. But good description and analysis is a stage of science that is much needed, and I view this effort as being an attempt along those lines. If I have been successful, the reader will recognize from his or her own experience many of the phenomena I describe, and that is, for me, an important level of validation.

Cambridge, Massachusetts Edgar H. Schein
June 1999

The Author

Edgar H. Schein is Senior Lecturer and Professor of Management Emeritus at the Sloan School of Management at the Massachusetts Institute of Technology. He received his B.A. (1947) from the University of Chicago in general education, his M.A. (1949) from Stanford University in social psychology, and his Ph.D. (1952) from Harvard University in social psychology.

His main research activities have taken him through many subject areas: from a study of the brainwashing of Korean and Chinese POWs to a study of management development and organizational socialization, and on to a deeper look at managerial careers. His interest in culture grew primarily out of clinical work with organizations in which culture became highly visible.

He is coeditor of the highly acclaimed Addison-Wesley series on organizational development (launched in 1969 with Richard Beckhard and Warren Bennis). His other recent books include *Process Consultation Revisited: Building the Helping Relationship* (1999), *Career Survival* (Jossey-Bass Pfeiffer, 1993), and *Organizational Culture and Leadership* (second edition, Jossey-Bass, 1992).

Schein was chair of the organization studies group of the Sloan School of Management from 1972 to 1981 and has consulted with a range of organizations around the world on culture, organizational development, and careers. A Fellow of the American Psychological Association and the Academy of Management, he is a member of the governing council of the Society for Organizational Learning and the founding editor of *Reflections: The SOL Journal*. He is considered a founder of the field of organizational psychology.

The Corporate Culture Survival Guide

Part One

Corporate Culture Basics

Chapter One

Why Does Corporate Culture Matter?

- Some Culture Lessons from Atari, Apple, IBM, DEC, Procter & Gamble, and "Acme Insurance"
- Culture Issues in Mergers, Acquisitions, and Joint Ventures
- Start-ups, Midlife, and Old Dinosaurs
- Where Does Culture Reside?
- The Bottom Line

Culture matters. It matters because decisions made without awareness of the operative cultural forces may have unanticipated and undesirable consequences. In the stories I tell in this book, the consequences were sometimes considered desirable and sometimes not. (In several cases of the latter, I have used fictitious names and indicated this by setting them in quotation marks.) The point is that they occurred, they could have been predicted, and in some cases they could have been prevented if culture had been taken seriously in the first place. The argument for taking culture seriously, therefore, is that one should anticipate consequences and make a choice about their desirability.

Some Culture Lessons from Atari, Apple, IBM, DEC, Procter & Gamble, and "Acme Insurance"

Many years ago, when Atari was preeminent in designing computerized games, they brought in a new CEO whose background was in marketing. His cultural background told him that the way to run a company was to get a good individual incentive and career system going. Imagine his chagrin when he discovered a loosely organized bunch of engineers and programmers whose work was so seemingly disorganized that you could not even tell whom to reward for what. Well, the CEO was sure he knew how to clean up that kind of mess! He instituted clear personal accountabilities and an individualistic, competitive reward system symbolized by identifying the "engineer of the month"—only to discover that the organization became demoralized and some of the best engineers left the company.

This well-meaning CEO had not realized that the essence of the creative process in designing good games was the unstructured collaborative climate that enabled designers to trigger each other's creativity. The successful game was a group product. The individual engineers shared an assumption that only through extensive informal interaction could an idea come to fruition. No one could recall who had actually contributed what. The individualized reward system gave too much credit to the engineer of the month named by the CEO, and the competitive climate reduced the fun and creativity.

Though the whole story at Apple Computer is not yet known, it is likely that John Sculley's tenure was bedeviled by similar issues. He tried to gain the respect of the technical culture that had spawned Apple's success but never succeeded; many of his efforts to make Apple a better company ran into resistance grounded in the culture that was there. It is probably no accident that eventually Apple turned back to one of its founders, Steve Jobs, to get it back on course.

If marketers are mismatched with technical cultures, how was it possible for someone like Lou Gerstner to come into IBM and successfully bring it back into profitability and economic health? Here too the story is not yet fully known, but taking a cultural perspective reveals a key fact about IBM. Tom Watson, Sr., the founder, was a salesman who became unhappy working for the autocratic John Patterson, founder of National Cash Register. Watson decided to create his own business-machines company—but note that he was a salesman, so he introduced many of the values and assumptions of a sales and marketing culture (Dyer, 1986). When IBM ran into difficulties some years ago, many insiders argued it was a marketing failure that accounted for the problems; hence getting a good marketing CEO was the correct way to regain their momentum. Although the technical side of IBM rose to eminence over time, the sales and marketing side has always dominated, so Gerstner fit right in.

The story of Digital Equipment Corporation is told in greater detail throughout this book, but for purposes of understanding how much culture matters it needs to be said at the outset that the very culture that made DEC a great company in a remarkably short period of time became dysfunctional as size, market conditions, and technology changed. Failure of the culture to adapt was at the root of the economic difficulties that eventually led to DEC's severe turnaround and ultimate acquisition by Compaq. Even though highly conscious of its culture, DEC was unable to change it from the inside.

Now to another kind of story. In the 1950s, Procter & Gamble decided they wanted to be a low-cost producer. A farsighted manager of manufacturing empowered a staff group to examine how one might organize plants to increase both productivity and worker satisfaction. With the help of organization development (OD) consultants such as Douglas McGregor and Richard Beckhard, they evolved a concept of a factory that depended much more on worker involvement and a reward system that emphasized multiple skills rather than hierarchical position or number of people supervised. The essence of the idea was to have a plant view itself as a business with suppliers and customers, and to run that business responsibly.

The staff group also realized that there was no chance of selling such a concept either to the union or to more traditional management types. They had to start with a new plant, hire their own plant manager, and teach him the new concept of a plant as a self-managing business. The "Augusta" plant was born and was soon highly successful. To proliferate this success, the staff group decided that potential managers of other new plants (and of the old unionized plants) would have to learn the new system in an apprenticeship capacity to ensure that they really understood it.

Over the next several years, a number of new plants started up, in each case with a manager who had apprenticed in the Augusta plant. The new operations worked well, but the unionized plants remained problematic. Some of the older-and-wiser ex-Augusta managers were then placed into those plants to begin the process of "changing the culture," although that was not the vocabulary used at the time. Each plant also had an OD manager reporting directly to the plant manager and who had been recruited from the employee ranks before being trained in organization development.

My work with one of these managers highlighted the problem. Until the union began to trust management, there was no chance of even discussing the new kinds of production systems that would allow for job trading and multiskilling—notions that violated some of the most sacred cows of trade unionism. In one plant, it took about five years for the union to decide that the manager could be trusted and to open discussion of a new kind of contract. After several more years, the union accepted the new system and saw that it was of benefit to all.

A few years ago, I attended a celebration marking the conversion of the last of P&G's unionized plants to the new system. The event occurred fifteen years after the launch of the Augusta plant, but a real culture change had been achieved in the manufacturing division. (No doubt a few years from now we will hear a similar story of how Jack Welch changed the culture of GE, and we will find once again that real change of this sort takes an intensive effort over many years.)

"Acme Insurance" (a pseudonym) illustrates the consequences of changing technology without analyzing the constraints of culture. A large insurance company decided to increase its competitiveness by rapidly evolving to the paperless office (Roth, 1993), with all major transactions to be done by computer in the very near future. To accomplish this change, they hired a talented manager of information technology who had a proven track record. She was given a tough target of converting the clerical staff to the new system within one year. Training modules were created to teach employees how to use the new system effectively. But the IT manager was not aware that the company was, at the same time, launching intensive productivity efforts that signaled to the employees that they had to get their normal work done in addition to whatever training they could squeeze in. The result was that the training was done in off hours and half-heartedly, and, worse, the IT manager was not told this because the employees feared senior management reprisal. At the end of the year, the IT manager announced that the paperless transaction system had been successfully installed. But she did not know that the employees were so poorly trained that it was taking them much longer to use the computers than it had taken to use paper. Productivity actually dropped. Failure to recognize some of the deep realities of their own culture caused this organization to waste tremendous amounts of money and effort for very little gain.

I observed a similar scenario in the back room of a large bank that installed computerized recordkeeping to reduce paper flow. Employees had data on their computer screens, but when a customer called with an inquiry there was never enough of the case history on a single screen for the employee to rely on. So the employees kept extensive backup folders, which they pulled out as needed. Whenever the IT-oriented manager came around, the folders disappeared and the employees pretended to be using only the computers. This was not a technology failure. It was failure to understand the subculture operating in the clerical group.

Culture Issues in Mergers, Acquisitions, and Joint Ventures

In these opening stories, culture is an internal matter and relatively invisible. When organizations that have developed their own cultures acquire each other, attempt to merge, or engage in various kinds of partnerships and joint ventures, the culture issue is more blatant and visible. However, surprisingly little attention is paid to culture before the new organization is created. As the new organization begins to function, people hear the rhetoric that "we will take the best from both cultures," but careful examination of the evidence points in a different direction.

It seems that in all cases where cultures have to be combined, there are three possible patterns: separation, domination, or blending.

Separate Cultures

The first possibility is that the cultures remain separate, as in conglomerates that allow subsidiary companies to retain their separate identities.

I was asked some years ago by the Swedish government to run a workshop for the senior executives of the government-owned Swedish industries to decide whether they should launch an effort to create a "common culture" across their various industries. After lengthy discussion of the disparate elements of shipbuilding, mining, bottled water, and so on, it was clear that a common culture was not only a bad idea but probably impossible to implement. The attendees did agree that the senior executives in each industry should be viewed as "corporate property" and be made available in whatever industry needed them. But even there, they decided it would be dangerous to remove such executives from the company in which they had achieved success.

Another Swedish case involved a lock company that was buying up local lock companies all over Europe but aggressively leaving them alone—and hiding its ownership in the belief that customers needed to maintain their confidence in the local lock companies they had always dealt with.

In these cases, the cultures need to be "aligned" in the sense of not working at cross purposes with each other. This is easy if the owners manage through limited financial linkages. It becomes more difficult in partnerships or joint ventures where the parents have different cultures. In a study of fifty-fifty (ownership) joint ventures with parents from different countries, very little evidence of initial blending was found (Salk, 1992). In a German-U.S. owned joint venture, the two groups of nationals clung to their own way of doing things for several years, until a local labor relations crisis forced them to work together and build some new ways of working that did actually draw on each other's expertise and way of doing things. In an Italian-Canadian joint venture, the two groups worked together for almost a decade without in any way integrating their cultures. Each group bad-mouthed the ways of the other. Because economic conditions were favorable, no incentive existed for making real efforts to integrate.

I worked with Ciba-Geigy in the late 1970s. It was some twenty years after Ciba had merged with Geigy, yet many managers still identified completely with the company from which they had come. They felt free to criticize the new company as not having taken advantage of some of their own "better" ways.

Dominant Culture

The second possibility in a combination is that one culture dominates the other. In some cases this is explicit, as when one company acquires another. When Intel bought a semiconductor plant from DEC, the new management announced that the plant would now operate by the Intel method—and that was that. When Hewlett-Packard bought Apollo, it coercively trained Apollo employees to adopt "the HP way."

Let me illustrate, using the HP-Apollo case. I worked with a group of computer division managers in Palo Alto and was told that the HP way required people to be nice to each other and reach consensus in group meetings. If you resisted too vigorously, they said, the boss would pull you aside later and tell you that you were not "a team player." Some months later, I was sitting next to a young woman who had gone to work for Apollo in Massachusetts; I asked her how she liked it. She said it was OK, but she worried that one could not really be outspoken or get one's point of view across. I asked her what would happen if she persisted in arguing for her view, and she said—literally—"The boss will pull you aside and tell you that you are not a team player!!!"

Does one see less domination in so-called mergers of equals? Or is every merger an acquisition—no matter the rhetoric about taking the best from each culture? In my own experience, one culture is always dominant, but this reality may not be visible for some time precisely because of the rhetoric. It will be interesting to watch how several current mergers work out from this point of view: British Petroleum and AMOCO, Chrysler and Daimler Benz, NYNEX and Bell Atlantic. In the study of fifty-fifty joint ventures (Salk, 1992) the one organization that did not remain culturally separate (a German-French partnership) was dominated by the French because the location of the organization was in France.

Blended Cultures

Possibility number three is that the cultures blend or integrate. Blending, taking the best of both cultures, is usually claimed to be the desirable outcome. What happens in practice is generally more complex and questionable. One level of blending is to create a new, superimposed set of values and sell them to the various cultural units. As we will see in later chapters, this only works under certain conditions. At another level, the new organization attempts to benchmark its various systems and procedures against each other and against externally perceived "best practices" to create and standardize new procedures across the resultant organization. One often hears that the new organization takes the accounting system from one parent, the human resource system from the other parent, and so on.

To balance power and maintain the image of merging, the chairman often comes from one company and the president from the other, or a succession system is announced that draws senior people alternatively from each organization. These moves preserve the public image of a merger, but it cannot be inferred from the standardizing of systems that the cultures actually blend. In fact, the often-seen resistance to changes in the new organization is almost always based on the fact that cultural issues have not been considered at all in making decisions about procedures. In one merger, it was found that a company paid very high salaries but aggressively resisted stock options and other forms of golden handcuffs because of a deep belief that one should neither provide promises of lifetime employment nor expect loyalty from employees. The other company had grown up with the belief that people needed to be developed as long-range resources and therefore had adopted a low-salary, high-stock-option and high-bonus system. There was no way to blend these two philosophies. One had to win out over the other. As the next case illustrates, sometimes winning brings disastrous results.

Two start-ups in a high-tech field merged after independent success over the first decade of their existence. The founder of Company A believed in teamwork, consensus, empowerment, and trusting employees to do the right thing; the founder of Company B believed that people must be highly disciplined, which required a well-functioning hierarchy. Each developed a management structure reflecting its beliefs. B acquired A to obtain all of the technical talent accumulated in A. Without giving the matter much thought, the president of B imposed his management system of clear hierarchy, tight controls, and tight discipline upon the newly acquired workforce—only to see a massive exodus, six months later, of the very people he had hoped to retain. It was an expensive lesson in the perils of ignoring culture.

Start-Ups, Midlife, and Old Dinosaurs

Culture matters in different ways according to the stages of organizational evolution. A *young and growing* company attempts to stabilize and proliferate the culture that it views as the basis of its success. The culture is the main source of the organization's identity and is therefore clung to with a vengeance, just as adolescents cling to their budding identities. Young organizations are also typically still under the control of their founders, which means the culture is more or less a reflection of the founder's beliefs and values. Even if success leads to broader acceptance of those beliefs and values across the whole population, one must recognize that a challenge to any cultural element is tantamount to questioning the founder or owners of the organization. Those cultural elements become sacred cows and are difficult to change. Culture change is therefore more a matter of evolving and reinforcing cultural elements, as is discussed in Chapter Five.

A *midlife organization* can be thought of as having had several generations of professional managers appointed by outside boards whose members are usually beholden to diverse stockholders. Most likely such an organization evolves into multiple units based on functions, products, markets, or geographies, and those units are likely to develop subcultures of their own. Thus the culture issue in the midlife organization is threefold:

1. How to maintain those elements of the culture that continue to be adaptive and relate to the organization's success
2. How to integrate, blend, or at least align the various subcultures
3. How to identify and change those cultural elements that may be increasingly dysfunctional as external environmental conditions change

There is at this stage a much greater necessity for accurate cultural assessment in order to maintain some parts of the culture while changing others. The organization also requires insight and skill to produce "managed" change of some cultural elements while maintaining the core. Culture change becomes transformation, because old cultural elements have to be unlearned. This is discussed in Chapters Six and Seven.

As *companies age*, if they do not evolve, adapt, and change elements of their culture, they grow increasingly maladapted and the culture becomes a serious constraint on learning and change. The organization clings to whatever made it a success. The very culture that created the success makes it difficult for members of the organization to perceive changes in the environment that require new responses. Culture becomes a constraint on strategy. An aircraft company that nearly went bankrupt with one of its commercial models became highly successful in the defense industry. New opportunities for commercial aircraft arose, but the board and senior management were unable even to contemplate going back into the commercial business because of their strong memories of the debacle several decades earlier.

The culture issue in the older company is how to engage in massive transformations, often under great time pressure to avoid serious economic damage. The process of transformation is basically the same as in the healthy midlife company, but the demands of time and the amount of change needed often precipitate drastic measures (usually labeled "turnarounds"). Rapid unlearning and letting go of things that are valued is for many employees too difficult; either they leave the organization or they are let go because they "resist change" too strongly. If the attempt to manage the change fails, the organization may go bankrupt—and start all over again, building a new culture with new management, or be acquired and find a new culture imposed on it.

Where Does Culture Reside?

Culture is a property of a group. Wherever a group has enough common experience, a culture begins to form. One finds cultures at the level of small teams, families, and workgroups. Cultures also arise at the level of departments, functional groups, and other organizational units that have a common occupational core and common experience. Cultures are found at every hierarchical level. Culture exists at the level of the whole organization if there is sufficient shared history. It is even found at the level of a whole industry because of the shared occupational backgrounds of the people industrywide. Finally, culture exists at the level of regions and nations because of common language, ethnic background, religion, and shared experience.

You as an individual, therefore, are a multicultural entity and display different cultural behaviors depending on what the situation elicits. But if you spend the bulk of your life in a given occupation and organization, you take on many of the cultural themes that others in the occupation or organization share. Thus the key to understanding whether a culture exists or not is to look for common experiences and backgrounds. Culture matters at this level because the beliefs, values, and behavior of individuals are often understood only in the context of people's cultural identities. To explain individual behavior, we must go beyond personality and look for group memberships and the cultures of those groups.

The Bottom Line

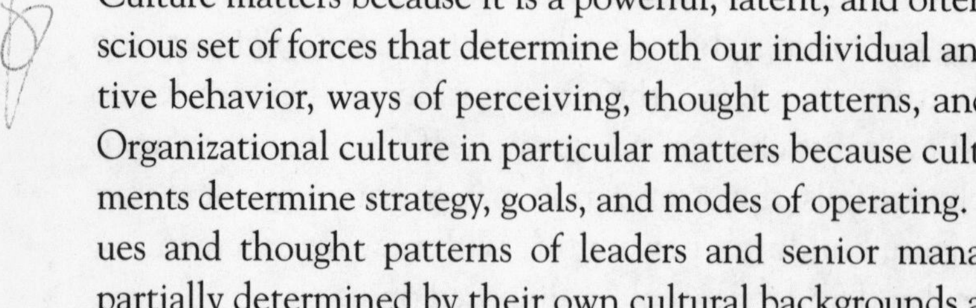

Culture matters because it is a powerful, latent, and often unconscious set of forces that determine both our individual and collective behavior, ways of perceiving, thought patterns, and values. Organizational culture in particular matters because cultural elements determine strategy, goals, and modes of operating. The values and thought patterns of leaders and senior managers are partially determined by their own cultural backgrounds and their shared experience. If we want to make organizations more efficient and effective, then we must understand the role that culture plays in organizational life. But what is culture, anyway?

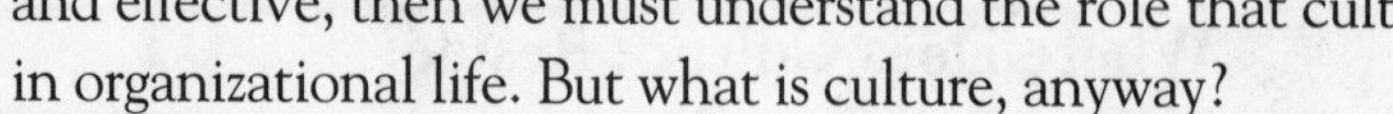

Chapter Two

What Is Corporate Culture Anyway?

- Three Levels of Culture
- Implications of Taking a Culture Seriously
- So, What Is Culture?
- The Bottom Line

The biggest danger in trying to understand culture is to oversimplify it in our minds. It is tempting—and at some level valid—to say that culture is just "the way we do things around here," "the rites and rituals of our company," "the company climate," "the reward system," "our basic values," and so on. These are all manifestations of the culture, but none is the culture at the level where culture matters. A better way to think about culture is to realize that it exists at several "levels," and that we must understand and manage the deeper levels (as illustrated in Figure 2.1).

Three Levels of Culture

The levels of culture go from the very visible to the very tacit and invisible.

Level One: Artifacts

The easiest level to observe when you go into an organization is that of artifacts: what you see, hear, and feel as you hang around. Think about restaurants, hotels, stores, banks, or automobile dealerships. Note your observations and emotional reactions to the

Figure 2.1 Levels of Culture

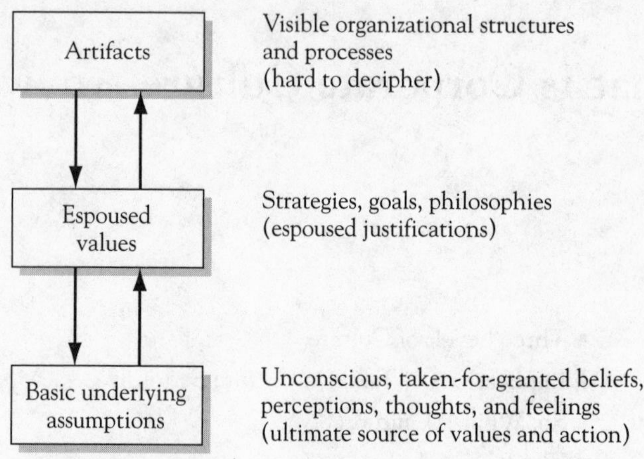

Source: Schein (1985).

architecture, the decor, and the climate, based on how people behave toward you and toward each other.

You can sense immediately that different organizations do things differently. In one organization (let's call it the Action Company), people are constantly in meetings with each other, there are no walls or closed doors, they dress informally, there is an intensity of feeling all around, and you get a sense of fast-paced action. In another organization, the Multi Company, everything is very formal. People are behind closed doors, conversations are hushed, dress is formal, and you get a sense of careful deliberation and slow movement. As a customer or new employee, you may like or dislike one or the other of these organizations; you may think to yourself that Action and Multi have different cultures. But you have to be careful. All you know for sure is that they have particular ways of presenting themselves and dealing with each other. *What you don't know is what this all means*.

In other words, at the level of artifacts culture is very clear and has immediate emotional impact. But you don't really know why the members of the organization are behaving as they do and why each organization is constructed as it is. Just by hanging around and observing, you cannot really decipher what is going on. You have to be able to talk to insiders and ask them questions about the things you observe and feel. That takes you to the next level of culture.

Level Two: Espoused Values

Imagine yourself to be a new employee or manager, offered a job at Action or Multi. Do you know enough about its culture from experiencing the artifacts and behavior patterns, or should you dig deeper? To dig deeper means to start asking questions about the things the organization values. *Why* do they do what they do? Why does Action create open office areas while Multi puts everyone behind closed doors? These questions have to be asked especially about those observed artifacts that puzzle you or that seem somehow inconsistent with what you would expect. For this purpose, you need to find insiders who can explain their organization to you. Anthropologists call them "informants" and depend heavily on such conversations to decipher what is going on.

The first things you learn are what I label in Figure 2.1 the organization's "espoused values." In Action, you may be told that they believe in teamwork, that you cannot get good decisions without arguing out what everyone's point of view is and obtaining buy-in from those who have to implement decisions. Therefore they must make it easy for people to communicate with each other. You may even be told that these values come directly from the founder of the company and that at one time in the company's history he had even forbidden having doors on offices. In this company, when they have meetings they tend to be free-for-alls and highly emotional. You may also be given some documents, pamphlets, or short papers that describe the company's values, principles, ethics, and visions. You are told that these documents are their culture and reflect their basic values: integrity, teamwork, customer orientation, product quality, and so on.

In Multi, you may be told that good decisions cannot be made without careful thought and that they value privacy and the opportunity for employees to really think things through before going into action. You may hear that this approach is necessary because the nature of their technology is such that careful individual research and thought is the only way to reach a good decision. In this company, meetings are formal and consist mainly of senior people announcing the decisions made and what now has to be implemented by junior people.

In Multi, you are also given various artifacts that purport to describe the company's values and principles. But now comes a surprise: you see that the list from Multi is practically identical to the one from Action. Multi is also customer-oriented, cares about teamwork, product quality, integrity, and so on. What is going on here? How can two organizations that espouse the same values have completely different physical layouts and working styles?

Having read a lot about culture in the popular press, you are now tempted to guess that these two organizations can be fit into a "typology." Clearly, Multi is a command-and-control kind of organization, while Action seems to be a flatter, team-based, network kind of organization in which people feel personally empowered. You may also have emotional reactions to these labels, based on your own past experience and values. So now you are ready to conclude that you understand these two cultures and can make a choice.

But don't give in to the temptation. You still do not understand either of these organizations at the deeper cultural level.

The typology may actually mislead you. All you know is that their artifacts are quite different yet paradoxically their espoused values are similar. Furthermore, the longer you hang around and the more questions you ask, the more you see obvious inconsistencies between some of the espoused values and the visible behavior. Both organizations espouse teamwork, yet both seem to have reward, promotional, and incentive systems that are highly competitive and individualistic. Both companies espouse customer orientation, yet neither is producing products that are particularly easy to understand or use, and neither has people who seem very polite or service-oriented.

What these inconsistencies tell you is that *a deeper level of thought and perception is driving the overt behavior.* The deeper level may or may not be consistent with the values and principles that are espoused by the organization. If you are to understand the culture, you must decipher what is going on at the deeper level.

Level Three: Shared Tacit Assumptions

To understand this deeper level, you have to think historically about these organizations. Throughout the history of the company, what were the values, beliefs, and assumptions of the founders and key leaders that made it successful? Organizations are started by individuals or small teams who initially impose their own beliefs, values, and assumptions on the people whom they hire. If the founders' values and assumptions are out of line with what the environment of the organization allows or affords, the organization fails and never develops a culture in the first place. But suppose that the founder of Action, who believes that people must argue things out and get buy-in on all decisions, creates a set of products that are successful. He attracts and retains others who come to believe the same thing (that one must always argue things out). If by this means they continue to be successful in creating products and services that the market likes, these beliefs and values gradually come to be *shared and taken for granted*. They become tacit assumptions about the nature of the world and how to succeed in it.

In Multi, let's suppose the founder is a scientist with some patents that spawned a very clear-cut production process resulting in goods and services that are much needed in the market and will be bought immediately once they are available. This founder wants a highly disciplined organization that can efficiently implement solutions that are already in his head or on the drawing board. He attracts people who like discipline and order, and as they succeed, they also come to take it for granted that hierarchy, discipline, and order are the only way to run an effective organization.

In other words, the essence of culture is these jointly learned values, beliefs, and assumptions that become shared and taken for granted as the organization continues to be successful. It is important to remember that they resulted from a *joint learning process*. Originally, they were just in the heads of founders and leaders. They became shared and taken for granted only as the new members of the organization realize that the beliefs, values, and assumptions of their founders led to organizational success and so must be "right."

To understand these two cultures, or any culture, you must unearth some of these assumptions that are operating yet are outside of members' awareness because they have come to be taken for granted. If you describe Multi to people at Action (and vice versa), they might tell you that the other bunch is "doing it all wrong."

Recall the stories that opened Chapter One. The new CEO of Atari did not understand the tacit assumption that products (computer and video games) result from a *group* effort. Sculley did not understand that in Apple the engineers assumed that only another engineer could really understand what they were doing. The IT manager introducing the paperless office at Acme Insurance did not understand the tacit assumption that getting one's normal work finished always had priority over training and that short-run productivity goals were always more important than long-range productivity improvements. DEC did not understand that the assumption that created rapid growth could become dysfunctional when they were larger and more structured. The P&G change team did understand that the unionized plants would not adopt a new method until they had developed trust in management and that the culture of these plants had been built up over decades on the assumption that management could *not* be trusted; they would first have to evolve to a new assumption and show that the new production system would actually benefit the unionized workers.

Implications of Taking a Culture Seriously

The implications of this way of thinking about culture are profound. For one thing, you begin to realize that culture is so stable and difficult to change because it represents the accumulated learning of a group—the ways of thinking, feeling, and perceiving the world that have made the group successful. For another thing, you realize that the important parts of culture are essentially invisible. Culture at this deeper level can be thought of as the shared mental models that the members of an organization hold and take for granted. They cannot readily tell you what their culture is, any more than fish, if they could talk, could tell you what water is.

Perhaps most important of all, you begin to realize that there is no right or wrong culture, no better or worse culture, except in relation to what the organization is trying to do and what the environment in which it is operating allows. General arguments of the sort you read in popular literature—about becoming more team-based, or creating a learning organization, or empowering employees—are all invalid unless they show how the basic assumptions on which these "new values" are based are adaptive to the environment in which the organizations have to function. In some markets and with some technologies, teamwork and employee empowerment are essential and the only way the organization can continue to succeed. In other market environments or with other technologies, tight discipline and highly structured relationships are the prerequisites to success. There is no best or right culture, as the Digital Equipment case example illustrates.

A Case Example: Digital Equipment Corporation

One example makes it clear how cultural assumptions that led to success in one environment can become dysfunctional as the environment changes.

When DEC started, it was, in effect, helping to create the computer market. No one knew for sure what the right products were and what customers would want in the long run. The deep assumptions on which DEC was built were that:

- One must start with smart and articulate people. But—
- Smart individuals must debate things in highly confrontational meetings because no one is smart enough to figure everything out alone, and things don't get implemented correctly anyway unless everyone buys into the decision. Yet—
- Even well-fought decisions can be wrong and the individual employee should not implement a decision if it makes no sense; instead he or she should "push back" to have the decision rethought. And in any case, do the right thing, even if it is insubordinate. To make all of this work, people had to feel secure with each other. So the assumption grew up that—
- We are one big family who take care of each other, and people cannot lose their membership even if they make major mistakes.

These assumptions working in concert with each other created an incredible sense of empowerment at all levels of the organization, and an atmosphere of involvement and commitment that created a highly successful company. This set of assumptions worked beautifully and is, in fact, the model on which many of the young computer companies built their organizations. You can see the origin of these assumptions and values in the engineering occupation, especially in the egalitarian pragmatic values of the electrical engineers who started many of these companies.

But reaching consensus by this means was a slow and often painful process. Successful negotiation and buy-in depended very much on the trust that developed in the "family," which was based on the members' being familiar with one another's styles. If the hardware developer asked a software counterpart whether the software would be ready in six months and got an affirmative answer, he would know whether this meant literally six months, or maybe nine months, or maybe not at all unless he kept pressuring his associate. Engineers and managers were *functionally familiar* with each other. They knew how to calibrate each other from working closely together over some period of time.

If a decision was made and down the road someone questioned it, it was her obligation to push back and do the right thing (as the deep assumptions put it). This process often unraveled decisions and improved them, but it took much longer and only worked if the functional familiarity among the players was high and they could trust each other not to bring up trivial issues. This model of how to work with each other was enormously successful and catapulted DEC into the Fortune 50.

But success brought growth, and as the organization grew, the debate was increasingly with strangers rather than trusted colleagues. Functional familiarity became rare and was replaced with formal contracts, checking on each other, and playing power games to make things happen. At the same time, the technology itself became more complex; this required a shift from an environment in which individual engineers designed complete products to one of large teams of engineers having to coordinate their efforts to build the complex products that were becoming possible and desirable. The highly individualistic, competitive, creative engineers found themselves increasingly having to coordinate their part of the design with others whose ideas they did not necessarily respect. The sense of involvement and commitment that characterized small projects was hard to sustain on large projects with multiple parts that had to be coordinated in a disciplined fashion. Whereas early in its history DEC engineers were king and dominated decisions, as the business matured other functions such as finance and marketing became more powerful; the result was conflicts among functional groups.

DEC's success attracted competitors, and as computers increasingly became a commodity, time-to-market and the cost of development and production became major factors. These external forces made the original assumptions about individual autonomy and empowerment increasingly dysfunctional. Intellectually, DEC leadership recognized these new forces and talked about shifting to smaller units in which the original assumptions that people believed in could be implemented. But for a variety of reasons the organization was not able to break the family down into small families. Yet remaining one larger unit increasingly created a political process in which baronies grew and mistrust replaced the functional familiarity on which the culture depended.

Central control became ever more difficult. Excessive costs, slow time-to-market, and inability to develop a coherent strategy in an increasingly complex market caused serious financial problems, until finally in the 1990s DEC had a major change in leadership and embraced a more hierarchical structure that would allow the discipline and efficiency the market now needed. (How this was accomplished is discussed in Chapter Seven on culture change.)

The lesson is that a good or right culture is a function of the degree to which shared tacit assumptions create the kind of strategy and organization that is functional in the organization's environment. If you were the kind of person who preferred the open, confrontational type of organization that DEC represented and went to work there in the 1970s, you would have had a blast. If you were there with the same mind-set in the 1990s, you might have found yourself out of a job.

So, What Is Culture?

Let me now summarize by going back to Figure 2.1.

What really drives the culture—its essence—is the learned, shared, tacit assumptions on which people base their daily behavior. It results in what is popularly thought of as "the way we do things around here," but even the employees in the organization cannot without help reconstruct the assumptions on which daily behavior rests. They know only that this is the way, and they count on it. Life becomes predictable and meaningful. If you understand those assumptions, it is easy to see how they lead to the kind of behavioral artifacts that you observe. But doing the reverse is very difficult; you cannot infer the assumptions just from observing the behavior. If you really want to understand the culture, you must have a process involving systematic observation and talking to insiders to help make the tacit assumptions explicit (see Chapter Four).

Practical Implication

So, what should you do differently tomorrow?

Take some time to reflect on your own concept of culture, and integrate into it some of the insights from this chapter. Think about the organization in which you work, and see if you can come up with some of its espoused values and shared tacit assumptions. Start by thinking about the artifacts around you. Locate things that puzzle you; ask an old-timer why they are that way. Try to see the culture as an outsider might (but for now try not to evaluate it or think about changing it).

The Bottom Line

The multilevel concept of culture makes it clear that culture is a complex concept that must be analyzed at every level before it can be understood. The biggest risk in working with culture is to oversimplify it and miss several basic facets that matter:

1. *Culture is deep*. If you treat it as a superficial phenomenon, if you assume that you can manipulate it and change it at will, you are sure to fail. Furthermore, culture controls you more than you control culture. You want it that way, because it is culture that gives meaning and predictability to your daily life. As you learn what works, you develop beliefs and assumptions that eventually drop

out of awareness and become tacit rules of how to do things, how to think about things, and how to feel.

2. *Culture is broad.* As a group learns to survive in its environment, it learns about all aspects of its external and internal relationships. Beliefs and assumptions form about daily life, how to get along with the boss, what kind of attitude one should have toward customers, the nature of the career in the organization, what it takes to get ahead, what the sacred cows are, and so on. Deciphering culture can therefore be an endless task. If you do not have a specific focus or reason for wanting to understand your organizational culture, you will find it boundless and frustrating.

3. *Culture is stable.* The members of a group want to hold on to their cultural assumptions because culture provides meaning and makes life predictable. Humans do not like chaotic, unpredictable situations and work hard to stabilize and "normalize" them. Any prospective culture change therefore launches massive amounts of anxiety and resistance to change. If you want to change some elements of your culture, you must recognize that you are tackling some of the stablest parts of your organization.

Chapter Three

What Is Corporate Culture Built On?

- The Popular View
- A More Realistic View of Culture Content
- Culture Content, Part One: Surviving in the External Environment
- Culture Content, Part Two: Integrating the Human Organization
- Culture Content, Part Three: Deeper Assumptions About Reality, Time, Space, Truth, Human Nature, and Human Relationships
- The Bottom Line

The Popular View

When you think about culture, chances are you identify some aspect of how the people in your organization relate to each other and how they do their jobs—"the way we do things around here." The most common view is that culture is about human relations in the organization. Most questionnaires that purport to assess culture deal with such issues as communication, team work, superior-subordinate relationships, the degree of autonomy or empowerment that employees feel, and the level of innovation or creativity that they display. Culture typologies built on these popular views talk about levels of "sociability" and "solidarity" (Goffee and Jones, 1998) or about "internal versus external focus" and "flexibility versus stability and control" (Cameron and Quinn, 1999). Culture-change programs talk about reducing the layers of supervision in the organization, creating lateral communication, building loyalty and commitment in the organization, empowering employees, and stimulating teamwork.

These views of culture are correct but dangerously narrow. Cultural assumptions in organizations do grow around how people in the organization relate to each other, but that is only a fraction of what culture covers. Culture-change programs that focus narrowly on how employees currently perceive their organization versus how they would like the organization to be are unlikely to work because they ignore other elements of culture that are more deeply embedded and may not even be noticed.

For example, a large insurance company hired a new CEO who concluded that among the company's main problems were lack of innovation and the degree to which employees did things by the book even when creative alternatives seemed to be available. A number of employee focus groups analyzed the organization's history; they revealed that past success was based on a tightly structured system of figuring out the best solution to any given problem, documenting the solution, putting all of the solutions into large manuals organized by every conceivable kind of problem that could arise, and systematically rewarding employees for using the rules written out in the manuals.

Over the years, employees learned that the road to success was to apply the rules. The number of manuals grew to cover every new situation that arose. Employees who did not like to work in this kind of rule-bound structured environment were encouraged to leave the organization; this eventually led to a workforce that was comfortable in the structured environment. Previous CEOs had glorified this system of working, and indeed it had been highly successful in building the company. It came to be taken for granted that the best way to work was to follow the rules in the manuals.

The new CEO saw that the company was in a changing environment and realized that many of the new situations the company would face could not be preprogrammed. Employees would have to learn to think for themselves as they faced a turbulent environment. He launched various campaigns to reward innovation (suggestion boxes, prizes for new ideas) yet got little response. He did not realize that the entire organization was built on the assumption that the correct way to do things was to follow the rules, and that over the years this assumption had become deeply embedded in all the layers of management and employees *because it was successful*. It was in the very fabric of how the organization operated, built into the reward system and the promotion system, and deeply influencing what kind of people were hired. For this organization to change its way of working would require a complete and realistic assessment of *all* aspects of its culture. What content areas would such an assessment have to cover?

A More Realistic View of Culture Content

Culture is the sum total of *all the shared, taken-for-granted assumptions that a group has learned throughout its history*. It is the residue of success. This abstract definition does not help you understand the content of culture, and the popularized view I described earlier can actually mislead you. To give you a more realistic view of what culture covers, look at Exhibit 3.1. It outlines the areas in which cultural assumptions make a difference. The first thing to notice is that cultural assumptions involve not only the internal workings of the organization but, more important, how the organization views itself in relation to its various environments.

Culture Content, Part One: Surviving in the External Environment

To survive and grow, every organization must develop viable assumptions about what to do and how to do it.

Mission, Strategy, Goals

For an organization to succeed in the sense of accomplishing its mission, surviving, and growing, it must fulfill what its various environments demand and afford. Most organizations evolve

Exhibit 3.1 What Is Culture About?

External Survival Issues
- Mission, strategy, goals
- Means: structure, systems, processes
- Measurement: error-detection and correction systems

Internal Integration Issues
- Common language and concepts
- Group boundaries and identity
- The nature of authority and relationships
- Allocation of rewards and status

Deeper Underlying Assumptions
- Human relationships to nature
- The nature of reality and truth
- The nature of human nature
- The nature of human relationships
- The nature of time and space

assumptions about their basic mission and identity, about their strategic intent, financial policies, fundamental way of organizing themselves and their work, way of measuring themselves, and means for correcting themselves when they are perceived to be off target.

When the organization was first created, its founders and early leaders had a strong sense of mission and identity—what they are trying to be, what product or market they are trying to develop, who they are and what justifies them. To raise money, they had to develop a credible story around these questions, and the first set of employees needed to buy into and believe the story even if they knew initially that it was a risk and might not work out. But if it did work out and the organization succeeded, the founders and the employees would begin to form shared assumptions around those initial beliefs and over time come to take them for granted. The deep sense of mission and identity may be so taken for granted that it surfaces only if some event violates it and thereby brings it to consciousness.

An example from the Swiss company Ciba-Geigy illustrates the point. In the mid-1970s, C-G consisted of four major product divisions (dyestuffs, industrial chemicals, agricultural chemicals, and pharmaceuticals) and many country units. Historically the company traced its roots to the dyestuffs business and the important discoveries made in the R&D labs that led to new products in the agricultural and pharmaceutical domains. The company recognized that its strength was in R&D and that it had remained profitable largely because of patent protection. Leadership recognized that as patents expired and competition in each market grew, C-G needed to improve marketing and reduce costs.

Thus far, this story may seem like fairly traditional evolution; so, where does culture come in?

To improve marketing skills, C-G empowered its U.S. subsidiary to purchase a consumer goods company because organizations of that kind learn how to do sophisticated marketing. They purchased Airwick, a maker of air fresheners, carpet cleaners, and other products to remove unpleasant odors. For a number of years, Airwick struggled along but gradually became profitable not only in the United States but in various European countries where it developed subsidiaries.

At that time, I was working with the C-G corporate executive committee in running an annual meeting of its top forty or fifty functional, divisional, and country managers. In one of the meetings, the president of the U.S. subsidiary was reporting on the progress of Airwick and showing videotape of a particularly successful advertising campaign that introduced a new product, Carpetfresh. The ads showed a housewife sprinkling Carpetfresh powder on her rugs and a minute or so later vacuuming it up, to illustrate how easy the product was to use.

I was sitting next to a member of the executive committee, a man who had developed several of C-G's major chemical products and who saw himself as an important strategist in the company.

Watching the videotape, he began to squirm in his seat, showed signs of great tension, and finally leaned over to me and said in a loud whisper, "You know, Schein, those aren't even *products*."

In that moment, I glimpsed his image of what C-G was all about. He saw it as a company producing "important products" that combated starvation (industrial pesticides enabled third-world countries to grow crops) and saved lives (pharmaceutical products were geared to curing major diseases). In that context, and with that sense of mission, how could one possibly view an air or carpet freshener as worthy of being deigned a "product"? How could one possibly want to associate with such a trivial matter? This man's self-image was violated by C-G's association with Airwick—never mind that the whole idea was to learn something about marketing and that Airwick was beginning to show good financial results.

Some months later, I learned of another way in which this corporate self-image impacted their learning process. The European division of Airwick was based in Paris, and that office hired a very talented woman to be chief financial officer. They reported with pride that they were beginning to break the gender barrier in their promotional policies, and she was a prime example.

However, she left some months later and related the following incident. In organizing Airwick's European operation, she needed a more efficient and speedier accounting system than what C-G was using. As the story goes, she went to the corporate head of accounting in the Basel headquarters and requested permission and funds to institute the new system, only to be told, "Mrs. Smith, I think you will find that our accounting system has been quite adequate to the task for one hundred years or so, and it should certainly be adequate, therefore, to your tasks." Needless to say, she left and Airwick managers were forced to bootleg systems in secrecy that would meet their needs.

The cultural moral of this story is that an acquisition strategy has to fit the existing culture. Even though the purpose of the acquisition was to learn marketing from a consumer-goods company, this particular set of products was giving C-G cultural indigestion. C-G's sense of mission and self-image were violated by these "nonproducts," even though Airwick was beginning to show profit in many countries. To deal with their discomfort, the executive committee appointed a senior Swiss manager to evaluate the future of Airwick over a period of several years and recommend what C-G should do with it. From a cultural perspective, it was obvious that he would eventually recommend that they sell Airwick—which is what they did. At the same time *they reaffirmed their self-image* of only making acquisitions of companies that were based on sophisticated technology. At subsequent annual meetings, it was stated explicitly that C-G should only buy companies with a strong technical base. Culture was driving the acquisition strategy.

C-G managers may or may not have recognized that they were dealing with culture, and that they held deeply embedded assumptions about who they were, what kinds of things qualified as products, and what acquisition strategy was OK or not OK. We tend to think that we can separate strategy from culture, but we fail to notice that in most organizations strategic thinking is deeply colored by tacit assumptions about who they are and what their mission is.

Over its history, any organization learns a great deal about what kinds of strategies work and what ones do not. Such strategies are about types of products and services, types of markets, level of quality desired, level of price that the customer base will accept, and so on. These points are reflected in the first category in Exhibit 3.1: the basic mission of the organization, its strategic intent, and the goals derived from the mission and strategy. This category of culture is so central that it warrants another example to illustrate how these culture dynamics work.

Early in the history of Digital Equipment, the mission was to bring efficient computing to the scientifically minded user, offer distributed computing power to organizations, and show the world the power of a midsized computer. Its product strategy, concept of who the customer was, pricing, and decisions about level of quality all were driven during the company's high-growth phase by these strategic goals. The degree to which they came to be taken for granted and thus part of the culture at DEC could be measured by the difficulty the company had in designing a product to compete with IBM's Personal Computer. At some level, DEC engineers did not really respect the "dumb user" for whom a low-cost, user-friendly PC would have to be designed; all of their past success had been with sophisticated users who were perfectly willing to do some of their own programming. The high technical standards and quality of DEC products also made them more elegant than they needed to be and more expensive, hence not very competitive in the new PC market.

Several cultural forces conspired to make the DEC entry into the PC world a basic failure. First was the deep assumption that the engineers basically did not care much about the dumb user. Second, smart people should be empowered to do the right thing. Three engineering managers with very strong ideas about the PC proposed potential products, named the DECmate, the Pro, and the Rainbow. At this point in its history, DEC was already fairly large and differentiated, and the engineering managers all had their own power base and strong convictions that their product would win in the marketplace. They were themselves products of the DEC culture.

A third cultural assumption that came into play was that if one could not make a clear internal decision, "let the marketplace decide." A tradition had grown up in the company that having internally competing groups was healthy; the marketplace would reveal which was the best product. DEC had been successful with this internal-competition approach and hence did not question it. It was OK to have three competing PC projects.

But the cultural assumption that each manager and employee was obliged to "do the right thing" led to another problem. Ken Olsen, the founder, and other managers believed that the three proposed products were over-engineered, too elegant, and too expensive. Yet no one, not even Olsen, could convince the engineering managers to scale down their products. In the DEC culture, one could not order the three groups to do things differently; one could only try to convince them. In the end, all three products failed competitively even though each claimed to be an excellent PC. The story highlights how a strategic failure in the product-development arena can only be understood in the context of culture.

Practical Implication

Ask yourself and others these questions:

- What is the fundamental mission of your organization? What is its reason for being? What justifies its existence in the larger scheme of things?
- How does your organization's strategy and the goals derived from it fit that mission?
- Where did this strategy and set of goals come from? Is the strategy completely based on formal reasoning and logic, or is it partly a product of the beliefs and biases of the organization's founders and leaders?

Means: Structure, Systems, and Processes

How an organization decides to implement its strategy and goals is the next level of culture content. The formal organizational structure in one company may be very tall, steep, and multilayered; *if they succeed* with this structure, they come to believe that it is the correct way to organize. In another organization, the founder creates a flat structure with many overlapping committees and task forces; here too, *if they succeed* they believe just as strongly that theirs is the correct way to organize. The degree to which the structure is adapted to the task to be performed and the nature of the environment in which the organization operates creates the shared tacit assumptions about how to organize. Glib labeling of an organization as a command-and-control type or a flat-network type reflects this category, but note that such labels describe not the whole culture but only one small aspect of it.

The complexity of cultural analysis is also revealed in this category in that an organization can have a shared mission and strategic intent, yet units may organize themselves differently in their efforts to achieve it. Subcultures are thus created within the organization's overall culture. As organizations grow and differentiate themselves into functional, product, market, and geographically based units, they also develop subcultures around each of these bases. Subcultures may be highly functional and efficient, because the parts of the organization have to succeed in different kinds of environments.

For example, in the 1960s a large aerospace company, Northrop, prided itself on its egalitarian structure; there were few levels and few rules throughout its production units. During a workshop to analyze their culture, a group of senior managers could not figure out why Northrop's headquarters organization in Los Angeles seemed to violate this culture by being multilayered and very rigid. There were three levels of dining rooms, all kinds of rules about dress and demeanor, rigid adherence to hours of work, and so on. They finally realized that the culture of the headquarters organization had developed this way because its primary customer was the Pentagon, and the military visitors to the company were used to a system in which status, dress codes, rank, privileges, and so on were all very well defined.

In their factories, though, a completely different set of assumptions grew up around the technology; it was complex, required a high degree of teamwork and mutual trust among employees, and defined rules in terms of quality of work and getting the job done. There were no time clocks; hours were determined by the nature of the task; the selection and promotion system encouraged hiring of relatives because it was easier to develop trusting relationships in a family atmosphere; and status was determined by knowledge and skill level, not by formal title. Once the group recognized that the tasks of factory and headquarters differed, they realized that it was appropriate for these units to develop distinct subcultures.

Recall from Chapter One how Procter & Gamble restructured the manufacturing division into a set of autonomously self-managed plants to achieve the shared strategic intent of becoming a low-cost producer while maintaining high quality. In their marketing, sales, and financial divisions no such structures emerged, showing that different means of accomplishing a shared strategy can coexist. Similarly within DEC's very egalitarian environment, there existed a service organization that was highly structured, authoritarian, and disciplined because in the service environment only such a structure could deliver efficiently what the customers required.

Every organization that succeeds develops a way of structuring work; defining the production and marketing processes; and creating the kinds of information, reward, and control systems it needs to operate effectively. As these systems continue to work, they are taken for granted as the way to do things, and an employee who moves from one company to another finds it difficult to learn how to work in the new environment. It is for this reason that once organizations have strong cultures, they prefer to promote from within. It is often too difficult to train an outsider in "how things are done around here."

Practical Implication

Ask yourself and others:

- How did your own organization develop its approach to meeting goals?
- How and why did it develop the kind of structure that it has? Do the formal structure and the design of how work gets done

largely reflect the beliefs of the founders and leaders of the organization?

- To what extent are the means used in the functional and geographic divisions the same (or different)?
- Is there evidence that your organization has strong subcultures within it? What are they based on?

~

Measurement: Error-Detection and Correction Systems

The third cultural issue seen in Exhibit 3.1 concerns how the organization measures itself, detects errors, and corrects them. Organizations evolve different mechanisms for deciphering the environment: frequent debriefing of the salesforce to determine what is going on "out there," formal marketing surveys, creating departments whose job it is to find out what is going on and bring the information into the organization, and others. The CEO, the salesforce, the purchasing department, the R&D unit, and the marketing department all have windows to the environment, but every company develops its own ways of using them and, if successful, comes to believe that theirs are the correct ways.

For most business organizations, financial performance is the primary error-detecting mechanism, but cultural assumptions dominate what kind of information is gathered and how it is interpreted. For example, some companies go almost exclusively by the stock price as the indicator of how they are doing. Others look at debt-to-equity ratios, cash flow, or market share. In each case, cultural assumptions arise from the indicators that work best. If the organization is functionally organized, it may also develop a subculture around the finance function, and actual conflicts may develop between finance, production, engineering, and marketing over which indicators to use in assessing company performance.

What is defined as a significant variance or an error itself varies from company to company and becomes embedded in cultural assumptions. One story about Levi Strauss has it that they were able to make major changes by declaring a crisis whenever the profitability index dropped by 0.5 percent. What is culturally significant in this story is not that they responded to such a small variance but that employees accepted management's definition that this was indeed a crisis.

Error correction, like error detection, reflects the history of the company and the personalities of its founders. Harold Geneen became famous for the way in which he measured the performance of ITT and how he rewarded or punished achieving goals or failing to do so. The culture of ITT undoubtedly came to reflect his managerial style. Many organizations develop what has come to be labeled a "blaming culture." Managers tend to be trained to think in terms of simple cause-and-effect; they need to feel in control, and the broader managerial culture makes a sacred cow out of individual accountability. Given this way of thinking, if things go wrong the obvious response is to find out who is to blame, who is responsible, who is accountable.

But companies differ markedly in how they respond to what they find out. In some organizations, once blamed a person is instantly dismissed. In other organizations, particularly those having grown around strong paternalistic and lifetime-employment values, this person may not even be told he or she has been blamed but is simply taken off the fast-track career ladder, given less-important assignments, and in other ways punished by having career opportunities permanently limited.

A third pattern that was evident in DEC was to be "put into the penalty box." Since everyone belonged to the family, no one could lose membership (a job), but you could lose your assignment on a project and be forced to find another assignment on your own. If you found another job in the company and did well in it, you were celebrated as a case of successful "rehabilitation." Underlying this system was an important assumption about people: if someone fails, it is because of a mismatch between the person and the job; the person is always OK, but the person-job match may not be.

This assumption made it clear how much people were valued, but it also made it clear that everyone had a great responsibility to manage their own careers and to speak up if there was a mismatch.

A fourth system of error correction used by many organizations attempts to avoid personal blame, instead seeking the root or systemic cause of the failure. The U.S. Army's program of "after action reviews," project postmortems, and other kinds of reviews attempt to build more learning into the process instead of blame. Note, though, that such systemic reviews do not work if the culture is strongly individualistic and competitive because people will not open up negative information about themselves and each other. If the organization develops a blaming culture, employees disassociate themselves from a failed project as quickly as possible and are reluctant to engage in a postmortem because it might reveal that they are in some way to blame. Only if enough trust and teamwork is built up over time, and only if that way of working succeeds, does systemic error analysis and correction work and become acceptable.

Practical Implication

Ask yourself and others:

- What are the error-detection systems in your organization? How do you discover that you are not meeting goals and targets?
- What do you do about it if you discover that some important goals are not being met?
- Are there variations among parts of the organization in how they measure themselves and what they do about the results? Can you see evidence in such variation of important subculture differences?

I have tried to show you in these last few pages that culture is heavily implicated in the basic mission, strategy, means, measurement, and remedial systems of the organization. Culture is not just about people and how we manage them. It is not just about teamwork or reward systems. Cultural assumptions develop over time regarding the core fabric of the organization and its basic mission and strategy. If you fail to take these parts of the culture into account when trying to change other parts of the culture, you will discover that the other parts do not respond as you hope they will.

Culture Content, Part Two: Integrating the Human Organization

The popularized view of culture focuses on the relations among the people in the organization, the incentive and reward systems, the degree of teamwork, superior-subordinate relationships, communication, and all the other processes that make the workplace more or less productive and pleasant. The cultural assumptions that grow up around these areas are, of course, critical. But they interact with the externally oriented assumptions we have reviewed (and listed in the first part of Exhibit 3.1) and thus cannot be treated in isolation, as so many culture audits imply can be done.

Common Language and Concepts

The most obvious manifestations of culture are common language and common ways of thinking. We see this most clearly at the national level, when we travel and find out how difficult it is to get along in other countries if we do not know the language or how the locals think. On a trip to southern France many years ago, I found myself in a small rural post office in a line waiting to buy some stamps. Just as it was my turn, a man came into the post office and started to talk to the clerk, interrupting my hesitant French request. To my surprise, the clerk turned her attention to the man and dealt with his issue for several minutes before returning to my request. When I told this story later to my French friends, they laughed and said: "You know Ed, the situation is even worse than you imagine. The clerk was going by the principle that she will deal with whoever's agenda she considers most important. By your letting the intruder capture her attention, you were displaying to the entire post office your low sense of self-esteem." Evidently what I should have done was to loudly and firmly recapture the clerk's attention instead of standing by in silent resentment.

The organizational equivalent of such events occurs when new employees try to figure out how to dress, how to talk to their boss, how to behave in group meetings, how to decipher all the jargon and acronyms that other employees throw around, how assertive to be, how late to stay at work, and so on. One reason it takes time before one can become productive in a new organization is because so many of the norms, ways of working, and ways of thinking are unique to that organization and have to be learned by trial and error.

For example, in DEC "real work" was defined as debating things out with others and getting buy-in, whereas in C-G real work meant thinking things out by oneself. At one point in DEC history, management decided they needed to speed up the process of cultural learning, so they launched a series of what they called "boot camps" for new employees in which newcomers and old-timers were taken off site to spend several days with a facilitator. The boot camp provided opportunities for the old timers to talk about the DEC culture and for newcomers to ask questions about all the things puzzling them in their new work environment.

Practical Implication

Ask yourself and others:

- Does your organization use special jargon or acronyms that you take for granted but that an outsider finds strange and undecipherable? What are some examples?

- What do your friends notice about your language and way of thinking that they associate with membership in your organization?
- If you have worked for more than one organization, what are the differences among them in how people talk and think?

Group Boundaries: Who Is In and Who Is Out?

Every organization develops ways of identifying degrees of membership, ranging from uniforms and badges to more subtle indicators such as who gets what parking slots, stock options, and other perquisites. As newcomers learn the language and ways of thinking, they find they are more often included in organizational events. An important stage of acceptance is when the newcomer is trusted enough to be told "secrets": information about what is really going on, who is in and who is out, what the company is really working on, details about the private lives of senior executives, and so on. With such membership comes the obligation to be more loyal, not to reveal those secrets to outsiders, work harder, and invest more of oneself in the organization. The shared tacit assumptions about membership and its obligations make up a significant portion of what we think of as the culture of an organization. But once again, remember: it is only one portion of the culture.

Practical Implication

Ask yourself and others:

- What are the badges of membership in your organization?
- Do you use special symbols or privileges to symbolize degrees of membership?

- Do you think about who is an insider, who is an outsider, and what this means in terms of your relationship to those people?
- Can you recall what it was like to enter your current organization?
- Have you brought anyone into your organization? How did you manage the process?

How Relationships Are Defined

Organizations differ in the assumptions they make about authority relationships and the degree of intimacy that is considered appropriate among members. Some organizations are aggressively egalitarian and minimize the psychological distance between bosses and subordinates. A hierarchy may exist, but subordinates are encouraged to use first names with their bosses, go around levels when it seems appropriate, and do the right thing even if it means insubordination (as was the case in DEC). In other organizations, the hierarchy is formally observed, relationships across levels are very formal, and it is inconceivable to go around levels or challenge the boss (as was the case in C-G). Both DEC and C-G thought of themselves as families, but for the former the family was a bunch of rebellious adolescents challenging their parents all the time, while for the latter the family was a set of "good" children who always did what their authoritarian parents told them to do.

Closely connected to authority relationships are assumptions about how open and personal relationships should be in the organization. In some organizations, employees are expected to be open about everything—even their feelings toward their bosses and each other. Such organizations are the exception. More common are norms that define clear boundaries about what can and cannot be talked about at work, and what can and cannot be said to the boss or to a subordinate. In some organizations, the assumption is that one leaves one's personal and family life at the door when entering the workplace. I know of a case where an employee's wife committed suicide, yet the employee continued to come to work as if nothing had happened. Others in the organization did not discover his tragedy for six months.

In DEC, people socialized with each other a good deal, especially because of the pattern of two-day off-site "woods meetings" where the work group would be together around the clock. In C-G, certain families got together for dinners, and at the annual meetings there would be one afternoon and evening planned for deliberately letting hair down by having the whole group engage in some novel sport that brought everyone down to the same level of incompetence, followed by an informal dinner. In Silicon Valley, many companies use social events such as parties, ski trips, weekends in San Francisco, and the like as rewards for their employees. In some instances, only the employee team is invited, while in others the spouses are included as well.

The point again is that each organization develops its own cultural assumptions about the degree to which employees are expected to become close to each other. I was told that at Apple people get very close on project teams, but that once the project is finished the friendships don't last. At HP, on the other hand, once friendships are formed they last even if someone leaves the company.

Practical Implication

Ask yourself and others:

- How appropriate is it to interrupt the boss when he or she is speaking?
- If you disagree with the boss, do you feel encouraged or discouraged to voice your disagreement face-to-face? Is it OK to disagree in front of others, or do you have to seek the boss out and disagree privately?

- Does your boss level with you about your performance, or do you have to guess how you are doing?
- If your boss asks you to evaluate him or her, how comfortable would you be saying exactly what you think and feel?
- How would your subordinates answer these questions in regard to you as the boss?
- Can you bring family and personal problems to work, or are you expected to keep them separate from work and private? Do you share with your colleagues or boss the problems you are having at home?
- If you and your partner are in a dual-career situation and you have to go home, say, to tend to a child, do you feel comfortable explaining the situation, or do you feel you have to invent an ironclad excuse to go home (perhaps taking a sick day or vacation day)?
- When you are at an informal event with your colleagues or boss, what kinds of things do you talk about? How comfortable are you in socializing with others in the organization? How many of them are friends whom you see regularly?

Again, keep in mind that there are no right answers. Cultures differ, and any given culture can work under one set of circumstances yet be completely dysfunctional under others.

How Rewards and Status Are Allocated

Every organization develops a reward-and-status system. The most obvious form is pay increases and promotion up the ladder. But organizational cultures differ in the meanings attached to these and other kinds of rewards. In some organizations and for some employees, promotions and monetary rewards such as salary, bonus, stock options, and profit sharing are the primary rewards and sources of status. In other organizations it is titles that matter, or the number of subordinates who report to you. In still other organizations and for some other employees (for example, engineers and scientists in the R&D function), the size of their project, the project budget, the degree of autonomy with regard to working hours, the visibility they have in the organization, the degree to which senior management consults them about strategic issues, their professional status outside the organization, and so on may be more meaningful as rewards and status symbols than pay and benefits.

One of the most difficult tasks facing the newcomer in an organization is to decipher the reward-and-status system. What kind of behavior is expected, and how do you know when you are doing the right or wrong thing? What kind of behavior is rewarded, and what kind punished? How do you know when you have been rewarded or punished? One of the most common complaints of employees and managers alike is "I don't know how I'm doing; I don't get any useful feedback." Performance appraisal systems are supposed to provide feedback, but most managers complain that they find it very awkward to be open in talking to their employees about their performance. To deal with this problem, some organizations are experimenting with complex feedback systems, such as "360 degree feedback," in which data are collected from a given employee's boss, peers, and subordinates; amalgamated; and then given back to the employee. But even in these cases it is surprising how often the person feels she cannot really "read" the signals as to whether she has been rewarded or punished, or neither. Of course, the degree to which such systems are open depends upon the cultural assumptions about the nature of relationships, as we have discussed.

Practical Implication

Ask yourself and others:

- In your work situation, what do you consider to be a reward or a punishment?
- What signals do you pay attention to in order to figure out how you are doing?

- When others get visible rewards, is it clear to you what they did to deserve them? When others get punished, how do you know they are being punished, and is it clear what they did to deserve the punishment?
- Can you identify the people with higher and lower status in your organization, and is it clear to you what their status rests on?

Once you answer questions such as these, you may think you have now deciphered your culture. Unfortunately, this too is still only a surface layer. Behind how organizations manage their external survival and internal integration issues are still deeper assumptions that need to be deciphered to understand culture fully.

Culture Content, Part Three: Deeper Assumptions About Reality, Time, Space, Truth, Human Nature, and Human Relationships

Organizational cultures ultimately are embedded in the national cultures in which the organization operates. Thus the deeper assumptions of the national culture come to be reflected in the organization through the assumptions and beliefs of its founders, leaders, and members. For example, Ken Olsen, the founder of DEC, was an American electrical engineer who believed profoundly in the U.S. values of competitive individualism, had a strong moral and ethical sense, and held a deep conviction that people could and should be trusted. These beliefs were reflected in all of the incentive, reward, and control systems that DEC developed. He also believed in individual responsibility and would get upset if he saw managers either failing to take responsibility or abdicating it to others, even if those others were their own superiors. As DEC evolved, it came to mirror exaggeratedly many of these aspect of U.S. culture.

Similarly, C-G grew up in the Swiss-German context and reflected many of the deep values and assumptions of that part of Switzerland: respect for authority, strong sense of responsibility and obligation to others who know more, loyalty to country and company, and individual autonomy (but combined with deep belief in collaboration and teamwork). I once was helping to design a workshop for C-G managers and proposed the "NASA moon survival" exercise, which shows how much better a group can reason than even the most knowledgeable individual. My Swiss counterpart wondered why I had bothered to suggest this, since most Swiss would take that conclusion for granted. In their view, it was only Americans who needed to learn the lesson that group results can be better than even the best individual results.

To examine the implications (for organizations) of such national culture differences, you need to go to a more abstract set of dimensions that have been developed by anthropologists for comparing cultures (Kluckhohn and Strodtbeck, 1961). These higher-order dimensions are also reflected in the artifacts you observe in organizations, but they are sometimes not reflected in the espoused values. For example, a company espousing teamwork does *not* necessarily operate from a deep belief that teams are better. In fact, the irony is that you often find that the espoused values reflect the areas where the organization is particularly *ineffective*, because it operates from contradictory cultural assumptions.

To get at the underlying assumptions at this level, you must see where the artifacts and values do *not* mesh and ask the deeper question of what is driving or determining the observed artifacts and daily behavior. For example, in the organization that espouses teamwork, if all of the incentive, reward, and control systems are based on individual accountability then you can safely identify an operative deep assumption that the individual really counts, not the team. In organizations that espouse employee empowerment, you sometimes discover that management assumes it has the right and obligation to command, own the financial information and decisions that affect the company, and treat the employees as a replaceable resource. These deeper assumptions are often difficult to decipher, yet they are the real drivers of how the culture works at the operational level.

Assumptions About the Relationship of Humans to Nature

Cultures differ in whether they believe that humans should have a dominant, symbiotic, or passive relationship to the natural environment. Thus in proactive Western societies we assume that humans can dominate nature, that anything is possible. The U.S. Marine Corps's slogan, "Can do," symbolizes this orientation and is reflected in a further slogan: "The impossible just takes a little longer." By contrast, in many Asian societies it is assumed that humans should blend into nature, or even make themselves submissive to nature. The natural environment is assumed to be more immutable, and the best way to be "human" is to blend with it.

In the organizational arena, these assumptions have their counterpart in notions that some organizations assume they will take a dominant market position and "define" the market, while others seek a niche and try to fit into it as best they can. Since business philosophy globally is to a large degree a reflection of modern Western society, the assumption has also grown up that it is advantageous to have a dominant position. There is research evidence supporting such assumptions, but this does not change the reality that in some societies the so-called correct way to define a business is to find a niche and blend in.

Practical Implication

Ask yourself and others:

- How does your organization define itself relative to others in its industry, and what are its aspirations for the future?
- Does it view itself as dominating, just fitting into a niche, or passively accepting whatever the environment makes possible?

Assumptions About Human Nature

Cultures differ in the degree to which they assume that human nature is basically good or basically evil, and in the degree to which they assume that human nature is fixed or can be changed. In his classic book *The Human Side of Enterprise* (1960), Douglas McGregor noted that U.S. managers differed greatly on this human nature dimension. Some assumed that humans were basically lazy and would work only if given incentives and controls—what he called Theory X. Other managers assumed that humans were basically motivated to work and only needed to be given the appropriate resources and opportunities; this he called Theory Y. McGregor also argued that the deep assumption basically determined the managerial strategy that a given manager would use. If they did not trust employees, they would employ time clocks, monitor them frequently, and in other ways communicate their lack of trust. The eventual result would be that the employees would react by becoming more passive; of course, once this happened, the managers would feel that their original assumptions had been confirmed. Much of what we call today command-and-control systems have at their root the assumption that employees cannot be trusted.

On the other hand, managers who believed that employees could and would link their own goals to those of the organization would delegate more, function more as teachers and coaches, and help employees develop incentives and controls that they themselves would monitor. McGregor observed that Theory Y managers were more effective; but again we must be cautious and note that different cultural assumptions may be appropriate to different kinds of tasks and circumstances.

A further important variation among cultures is the degree to which it is assumed that human nature is fixed or malleable. In most western cultures, especially the United States, we endorse the view that we can be whatever we choose to be, as illustrated by the thousands of *How to Improve Your . . .* books that proliferate in airport bookstalls. In other cultures it is believed that human nature is fixed and one must adapt as best one can to what one is.

Practical Implication

Ask yourself and others:

- What are the assumptions or "messages" behind the incentive, reward, and control systems in your organization? Do these systems communicate trust of employees, or mistrust?
- If you had to rate your organization on a 10-point scale (with 1 being totally Theory X, 10 totally Theory Y), how would your organization score? Would units of the organization reflect different assumptions?
- Do you believe that employees and managers can be developed, or do you basically have to select them for the right qualities? Which qualities are developable, and which ones are not?

Assumptions About Human Relationships

Is society basically organized around the group or community, or is society basically organized around the individual? If the individual's interests and those of the community (country) are in conflict, who is expected to make the sacrifice? In a groupist or communitarian society, as in Japan or China, it is clearly the individual who is expected to make the sacrifice. In an individualistic society like the United States, it is the group that must give because individual rights are ultimately believed to be the basis of society. Thus in the United States it is possible for any citizen to sue even the U.S. government, a concept that does not even exist in the minds of citizens of a strongly communitarian society.

Organizations mirror this dimension in the extent to which they emphasize company loyalty and commitment versus individual freedom and autonomy. In strongly paternalistic companies such as C-G, it was expected that the company would take care of you and in return you would be loyal to the company and make sacrifices when necessary. On the other hand, at Apple and many other Silicon Valley companies the assumption evolved that the company does not guarantee employment security and does not expect the employee to be loyal. Hewlett-Packard stands out in sharp contrast in having from the beginning espoused and practiced a more groupist paternalistic philosophy, symbolized most clearly by the 1970s incident in which everyone took a pay cut instead of laying people off. At the same time, in many of its work domains the individualistic assumption dominates in that rewards, incentive, and controls are all based on individual performance.

If one looks at U.S. organizations in general, the clearest indicator of individualism is the sacred cow of individual accountability. No matter how much teamwork is touted in theory, it does not exist in practice until accountability itself is assigned to the whole team and until group pay and reward systems are instituted.

Practical Implication

Ask yourself and others:

- How much does your organization reflect deep individualistic versus groupist assumptions?
- How are incentives, rewards, and controls organized? If teamwork is espoused, how does it work out in practice?

Assumptions About the Nature of Reality and Truth

In every culture, we grow up with beliefs and assumptions about when to take something as real and true. In modern Western society, we begin with the belief that truth is what our parents, teachers, and other authority figures tell us, but then gradually we are taught to trust our own experience and scientific proof. In fact, we end up making science itself another sacred cow, as reflected in the advertising industry's obsession with statistics, scientific testing, and purported proof ("Doctors recommend . . ."). Philosophically, we can think of this set of assumptions as ultimately pragmatic. We believe that which works.

But not all cultures are pragmatic in this sense. In many cultures traditions, moral principles, religious doctrines, and other sources of ultimate authority define more clearly what is to be regarded as real and true. As we all know, even in Western society there are many arenas in which we take religious and moral authority to be more real than pragmatic experience. DEC reflected the ultimately pragmatic assumptions: everything had to be fought out, and only ideas that survived the debate could be true enough to be worthy of testing. The test was again pragmatically symbolized by DEC's willingness to have parallel competing projects that would be tested ultimately in the marketplace. C-G, on the other hand, took it for granted that since its evolution was based on chemistry and research, those with education and experience in this arena were qualified to define what was true. Whereas at DEC every idea was battled out—even if it came from founder Olsen or technical guru Gordon Bell—at C-G if a high-status senior researcher with a Ph.D. proposed an idea then it was likely to be accepted.

Moral or religious principles come to dominate business decisions in some organizations, such as when, on principle, a company refuses to go into debt, or when personnel policies are governed by religious or moral principles. Thus in one organization lying is accepted as an inevitable consequence of politics, but in another organization the same behavior is severely punished on moral grounds. In a highly moralistic society, reality is often defined by the common moral code, whereas in a highly pragmatic society one ends up with some equivalent of the rule of law. In other words, the more pragmatic the society, the more the conflict-resolution mechanisms for what is true (what really happened) end up in a court of last resort that is based on common law and history.

Practical Implication

Ask yourself and others:

- If you think of one or two key decisions that your organization has made in the last several years, what were the decisions ultimately based on? How was information defined? What was treated as a fact versus an opinion? What facts were decisive in making a decision, and what ultimately did the decision rest on? Was it facts, or opinions? If opinions, whose opinions mattered, and what gave those opinions credibility?
- If you had to rate your organization's decision-making style (with 1 being completely moralistic and 10 being completely pragmatic), where would you place it on the scale?

Assumptions About Time and Space

Cultural assumptions about time and space are the hardest to decipher yet the most decisive in determining how comfortable we feel in any given environment. If we look at assumptions about time first, cultures vary in the degree to which they view time as a linear resource, once spent never to be regained (Hall, 1959, 1966). Time is money and is to be used carefully. In any given unit of time, only one thing can happen; hence we develop calendars and appointment books. In other cultures, time is more cyclical; it is considered OK to do several things at once, as when a senior person "holds court" and is able to process the needs of several subordinates at once.

Organizations differ in the meaning they attach to being on time or late. In Latin countries, being late might be regarded as fashionable and appropriate, while in northern European countries it is regarded as insulting. Arriving at work early and leaving late can have different symbolic meaning in different contexts; it could be taken as high commitment or as inability to be efficient.

In some occupations, schedules and time planning are critical to meet windows of opportunity or facilitate coordination. But in other occupations, such as biology or chemistry, time is measured more by how long things take.

Practical Implication

Ask yourself and others:

- What norms about time do you have in your organization?
- What does it mean to be late or early, or to come in early or leave early?
- Do meetings start on time? Do they end on time?
- When you make an appointment with someone, how much time do you feel is normal?
- Does it bother you to be doing two or more things at the same time?
- How does your organization react to missed targets or schedules?

Space, like time, has important symbolic meanings. Open office layouts imply that people should be able to easily communicate with each other, while private offices and closed doors symbolize the need to think for oneself. In some cultures, privacy means being literally out of sight behind closed doors. In other cultures it is considered private if you are out of hearing range, even if you are visible.

The normal distance that people stand apart from each other symbolizes the formality of relationships: the closer, the more the implication of intimacy. If someone with whom we do not feel intimate stands too close, we find ourselves being uncomfortable and backing up; if someone lets us move in more closely, we interpret it as willingness to become more intimate (as when we literally whisper secrets into someone's ear at very close range).

Where we place offices and desks symbolizes status and rank. Usually the higher the rank, the higher up in the building the office is located and the more it is surrounded by physical barriers to ensure privacy. The location and size of offices as well as the furnishings are in many organizations directly correlated with rank. We joke about status symbols such as wall-to-wall carpeting or having a window overlooking a nice view, but these jokes reflect serious cultural assumptions about the meaning of physical things in the environment.

Practical Implication

Ask yourself and others:

- How does the physical layout in your organization reflect working style and status?
- How do people express their rank through physical and spatial behavior?
- How do you organize the space around you, and what are you trying to communicate with how you do it?
- How is privacy defined in terms of physical layout?

The Bottom Line: So What Do You Do Differently Tomorrow?

The main lesson to learn in reading this far is that culture is deep, extensive, and complex. It covers all aspects of reality and human functioning. It influences how you think and feel as well as how you act, and it provides meaning and predictability in your daily life. So don't take it lightly, and don't think glibly about changing it. You yourself might not like the consequences of the very changes you are thinking about. But if things don't go right, if your organization is not achieving goals or you think you can do better, then you do need to get in touch with the deeper cultural assumptions that are driving you.

Starting now, become more analytical and reflective about culture. Put a hold on your impulse to take quick action. If you have been trying to make changes in how your organization works, you need to find out how the existing culture aids or hinders you. If you discover that some of your cultural assumptions are dysfunctional, figure out how to change them. What you have to look at next, then, is how to get at these assumptions systematically, beyond the kind of questions that I asked you to reflect on throughout this chapter. How do we assess culture? What is a culture "audit"? Can one determine culture with a well-designed questionnaire? These are the main questions of Chapter Four.

Chapter Four

So How Can You Assess Your Corporate Culture?

Culture assessment comes into play when an organization identifies problems in how it operates or as a part of a strategic self-assessment relating to merger, acquisition, joint venture, or partnership. By answering the questions in Chapter Three, you have begun this self-assessment. But your ability to decipher your own culture is still limited. What other techniques are available to you?

Should You Use a Survey?

Most managers are measurement-oriented. It is part of the culture of management. You probably want to know right away whether there are surveys available that allow you to measure your culture and put numbers on all of the dimensions reviewed in the preceding chapter. There are survey instruments and questionnaires that claim to measure culture, but in terms of the culture model that I present, they only unearth some of the artifacts, some espoused values, and maybe one or two underlying assumptions. They do not reach the tacit shared assumptions that may be of importance in your organization. Why is this so? Why has no one developed a reliable and valid culture survey?

Why Culture Surveys Do Not and Cannot Measure Culture

There are several reasons why culture questionnaires do not reveal cultural assumptions—and why, in fact, they cannot do so.

You Don't Know What to Ask

First, *you don't know what to ask about, or what questions to design*. Remember that culture covers all aspects of what an organization learns over its history. To design a questionnaire that grapples with all of the external and internal dimensions reviewed in Chapter Three (see Exhibit 3.1), you would have to write several hundred questions but still have no way of knowing which dimensions are the important ones in your organization. Some culture analysts claim they have isolated a limited set of relevant dimensions and designed surveys dealing with those dimensions; all of my experience tells me, though, that every organization has a unique profile of cultural assumptions that any questionnaire inevitably misses (see Hofstede, 1980, 1991; Cameron and Quinn, 1999; Goffee and Jones, 1998).

Surveys almost invariably deal with espoused values concerning working relationships. Do employees feel involved? Are communications open enough? Do employees feel they understand the company strategy? And so on. These may be important dimensions of the company's *climate*, and so they should be measured. The danger is that they become confused with culture. What if the important elements of the culture are instead the tacit assumptions about strategy, customers and markets, use of money, and other matters that may have little to do with the human relations in the workplace and are completely overlooked by the survey? For example, if a company has always operated without much debt and been successful, it may now assume that keeping debt low and cash balance high is the correct way to manage its finances. This assumption about managing finances can become a crucial part of its culture and hence shape all kinds of strategic and operational decisions. But there is no way of knowing ahead of time whether one should design finance-type questions into one's culture survey.

Asking About Shared Processes Is Ineffective

Second, *asking individuals about a shared phenomenon is inefficient, and possibly invalid.* It is not easy for anyone to access shared tacit assumptions, so the idea of using a questionnaire is based on faulty logic in the first place. Inasmuch as culture is a group phenomenon, it is far easier to elicit information in groups by asking broad questions about different areas of organizational functioning and seeing where there is obvious consensus among the members of the group. In the group, one learns not only what the areas of concern are but also the intensity of feeling about them, and thereby the centrality of different shared assumptions in the total cultural profile.

Furthermore, there is no way of knowing what a person answering a questionnaire reads into the questions, nor the attitude elicited by the usual promises of anonymity and privacy. Ironically, having to give employees an anonymous survey surrounded by all kinds of procedures to ensure that no one is identified says more about the deep assumptions of the organization's culture than any statistical analysis of the responses. Consider what is implied by the need to keep things anonymous, the threat of punishment if an employee gives negative information, and the secrecy surrounding the whole project. In contrast, doing a culture study by bringing focus groups together openly to discuss the values and shared assumptions operating in the organization sends a completely different signal.

What Employees Complain About May Be Unchangeable

Third, *the things employees complain about may not be changeable* because they are embedded in the culture. The survey does have some value in identifying whether the espoused values are being met or not, and in most cases the survey data can show areas where they are not being met. But to make the changes the employees desire, one then has to *do a "real" culture study* to see why the values are not being met and what has to change in the culture for them to be met.

For example, as has been pointed out, it is common for companies to espouse teamwork; surveys often reveal that employees wish there were more teamwork, more trust among employees, and so on. However, examining the artifacts typically shows reward-and-incentive systems that put a premium on individual accomplishment and competition among employees for the scarce promotional opportunities that are available. If the company really wants to become team-based, it has to replace those individualistic systems that have worked in the past and are deeply embedded in people's thinking. If it cannot or will not do that, the end result could well be a *drop* in morale as employees discover that what they hoped for is not happening.

In other words, what is often labeled the "desired culture" is a set of espoused values that may simply not be tenable in the existing culture. We can espouse teamwork, openness of communication, empowered employees who make responsible decisions, high levels of trust, and consensus-based decision making in flat and lean organizations until we are blue in the face. But the harsh reality is that in most corporate cultures these practices don't exist because the cultures were built on deep assumptions of hierarchy, tight controls, managerial prerogatives, limited communication to employees, and the assumption that management and employees are basically in conflict anyway—a truth symbolized by the presence of unions, grievance procedures, the right to strike, and other artifacts that tell us what the cultural assumptions really are. These assumptions are likely to be deeply embedded and do not change just because a new management group announces a "new culture." As we see in the later chapters, if such assumptions really are to change, we need a major organizational transformation effort.

How to Get at Your Own Culture

Another way to put this is to ask yourself, *Am I a unique personality, or just an example of a culture?*

This question has preoccupied psychologists and sociologists for a long time. The answer is that you are unique, the product of your own genetic makeup and particular experience of growing up. But in the process of growing up, you also become a member of cultural units that leave their residue in your personality and mental outlook. The most obvious manifestation is the language or languages you speak, which clearly you learn (they are not genetic) and which determine to a great degree your thought process and how you perceive the world. Beyond language are the many attitudes and values you pick up in your family, school, and peer group. It has been shown over and over again that kids show patterns of attitudes and values that are *systematically* different according to the community and socioeconomic strata in which they grow up.

So how do you access your cultural side? The most useful exercise is to ask yourself now, as an adult, what groups and communities you belong to and identify yourself with. Pay special attention to your occupational community (Van Maanen and Barley, 1984). If you are an engineer doing engineering work, chances are you have a whole set of assumptions about the nature of the world that you learned as part of your formal education and in your early job experiences. On the other hand, if you have always been interested in selling, took a business course in school, and are working your way along in a sales and marketing career, you probably hold assumptions reflecting that occupational community. Notice that as a salesperson you often disagree with engineers and may even get angry at their outlook, forgetting that you and they see the world through the differing lenses of your own cultural educations.

Your political beliefs, your spirituality or religion, and your personal tastes and hobbies all reflect the kind of groups you grew up in and belong to in the present. We know this intuitively and realize that we are a product of our environments. What a cultural perspective adds to this insight, however, is recognition that your current outlook, attitudes, and assumptions are also a reflection of *present* group and community memberships, and that one of the reasons you and others cling to your culture is that you do not want to be a deviant in the groups that you value. In other words, one source of strength for cultural assumptions is that they are shared and that the need to remain in the group keeps them active. To look ahead, let me say that when we advocate changing culture, we are, in effect, asking that entire groups and communities alter one of their shared characteristics. No wonder it is so difficult; no wonder people resist change so much.

Practical Implication

Think through what groups and communities you belong to. Rank them in terms of their importance to you in the present and in the future. For each group or community, list some key assumptions, attitudes, beliefs, and values it holds. Use the categories in Exhibit 3.1 as a guideline.

Allow yourself to be surprised by how much of your personality and character—your thought processes, perceptions, feelings, and attitudes—are shared with other members of the communities to which you belong. Though we operate in life as individual actors, we are far more embedded in groups than we realize.

Deciphering Your Company's Culture: A Four-Hour Exercise

Remember that cultural assumptions are tacit and out of awareness. Even so, this does not mean they are repressed or unavailable. If you want to access your organization's culture, get together with several colleagues (and maybe some newcomers to the organization), bring in a facilitator who knows a little about the concept of culture along the lines described here, and interview yourselves about those areas that seem to matter to the continuing success of your organization. The steps are as follows.

Define the "Business Problem"

Meet in a room with lots of wall space and a bunch of flipcharts. Start with a "business problem": something you would like to fix, something that could work better, or some new strategic intent. Focus on concrete areas of improvement, or else the culture analysis may seem pointless and stale.

Review the Concept of Culture

Once you agree on the *strategic or tactical goals*—the thing you want to change or improve—review the *concept* of culture as existing at the three levels of visible artifacts, espoused values, and shared tacit assumptions. Make sure that all the members of the working group understand this model.

Identify Artifacts

Start with *identifying lots of the artifacts* that characterize your organization. Ask the new members of the organization what it is like to come to work there. What artifacts do they notice? Write down all the items that come up. Use Exhibit 4.1 as a thought starter to make sure you cover all of the areas in which cultural artifacts are visible. You will find that as the group gets started, all the participants chime in with things they notice. You might fill five to ten pages of chart paper. Tape them up so that the culture's manifestations are symbolically surrounding you.

Identify Your Organization's Values

After an hour or so, shift gears and ask the group to list some of the *espoused values* that the organization holds. Some of these may have already been mentioned, but list them on pages separate from the artifacts. Often these have been written down and published. Sometimes they have been reiterated as part of the "vision" of how the organization should be operating in the future to remain viable and competitive.

Compare Values with Artifacts

Next, *compare the espoused values with the artifacts in those same areas*. For example, if customer focus is espoused as a value, see what systems of reward or accountability you have identified as artifacts and whether they support customer focus. If they do not, you have identified an area where a deeper tacit assumption is operating and driving the systems. You now have to search for that deeper assumption.

To use another example, you may espouse the value of open communication and open-door policies with respect to bosses, yet you may find that whistle-blowers and employees who bring bad news are punished. You may have detected, among your artifacts, that employees are not supposed to mention problems unless they have a solution in mind. These inconsistencies tell you that at the level of shared tacit assumption your culture is really closed, that only positive communications are valued, and that if you cannot come up with a solution you should keep your mouth shut.

As a general principle, the way to deeper cultural levels is through identifying the inconsistencies and conflicts you observe

Exhibit 4.1 Some Categories for Identifying Artifacts

- Dress codes
- Level of formality in authority relationships
- Working hours
- Meetings (how often, how run, timing)
- How are decisions made?
- Communications: How do you learn stuff?
- Social events
- Jargon, uniforms, identity symbols
- Rites and rituals
- Disagreements and conflicts: How handled?
- Balance between work and family

between overt behavior, policies, rules, and practices (the artifacts) and the espoused values as formulated in vision statements, policies, and other managerial communications. You must then identify what is driving the overt behavior and other artifacts. This is where the important elements of the culture are embedded. As you uncover deep shared assumptions, write them down on a separate page. You will begin to see what the patterns are among those assumptions, and which ones seem to really drive the system in the sense that they explain the presence of most of the artifacts that you have listed.

Repeat the Process with Other Groups

If the picture formed from this meeting is incomplete or muddy, *repeat the process with one or more other groups*. If you think there might be subgroups with their own shared assumptions, test your thought by bringing together groups that reflect those possible differences. If you need to repeat this process several times (using about three hours each time), you are still far ahead of the game in terms of time and energy invested relative to doing a major survey by either questionnaire or individual interviews. The data you obtain are also more meaningful and valid.

Assess the Shared Assumptions

It is now time to assess the pattern of shared basic assumptions you have identified in terms of *how they aid or hinder you* in accomplishing the goals you set out in the first step of this process (defining the business problem). Since culture is very difficult to change, focus most of your energy on identifying the assumptions that can *help* you. Try to see your culture as a positive force to be used rather than a constraint to be overcome. If you see specific assumptions that are real constraints, then you must make a plan to change those elements of the culture. These changes can best be made by taking advantage of the positive, supportive elements of your culture. This change process is explained and illustrated in Chapters Six and Seven.

Do You Need an Outside Consultant to Do the Assessment?

In my experience, the group that is deciphering the culture needs a facilitator who understands the concept of culture as I have laid it out here, and who is not a member of the group or department doing the culture self-study. This can be an outside consultant, but it does not have to be. Many organizations have internal organization development professionals who can play the outsider role effectively. Sometimes an organization hires me to train the insiders on this process and then does the self-study with its own trained staff. The facilitator must be someone who can create the setting, provide the model, and keep asking provocative questions to keep the self-study group moving forward until some important shared tacit assumptions of the culture are brought to consciousness. This process is illustrated in the next few cases.

Four Case Examples and Analyses

If you are a "one minute" manager, and if you think you now understand this process, you can skip the cases and go straight to Chapter Five—but be careful about choosing to skip them. In my experience, it is the concrete examples and cases that really give you the insight into what culture is all about. As you read the cases, imagine yourself in one of several roles:

- You are the change agent who decides that your organization needs some self-assessment
- You are a member of one of the assessment groups going through the process
- You are a facilitator who is running this exercise for another organization, or some part of your own organization in the outsider role

Imagine how this exercise feels from all these points of view.

"Beta Oil"

This case illustrates the culture-deciphering process in a project that did not initially involve the total corporate culture directly but instead required that we clarify the culture to accomplish the goals of the project.

"Beta Oil" restructured its internal engineering operations by combining all of engineering into a single service group. Previously, the eight hundred engineers involved had been working for various business units, refineries, and exploration and production units as members of those organizations. In the new, centralized organization, they would work as consultants to those organizations and charge for their services. The formal rules were that all engineering services would be charged for, with the fees to the various internal customers sufficient to cover the costs of running the eight-hundred-person engineering unit. The business units that would "hire" engineers to build and maintain the exploration, production, refining, and marketing activities could either use the internal central group or go outside for those services. However, the engineering services unit could only sell its services internally.

I learned all of this from the internal OD manager assigned to this central services group, whom we will call Mary. She was charged by the manager of the unit with forming a "culture committee," whose mission was to define the so-called new culture of this unit as it evolved into its new role. It was recognized that the individual engineers faced a major change, from being members of a business unit to being freelance consultants who now had to sell themselves and their services, and who had to bill for their time according to a preset rate. Mary recognized that creating a new culture in this unit was intimately connected to the existing culture in the larger company, since both the engineers and their customers were long-time employees of Beta Oil. It was also recognized that the engineers were coming from subcultures, and one problem was to create a single culture for the new unit.

After several hours of conversation with Mary to plan how the culture committee could function effectively and what kinds of intervention might be needed, we decided that we had to do an assessment of Beta's *corporate* culture. I was to be the facilitator, and she would bring together a group of fifteen or so engineers and managers from the unit. The workshop devoted four hours to a discussion along the lines described above:

1. Polling the group to get consensus on the business problem: the evolution of a new way of working and new values for the service unit in the context of the realities of the Beta culture
2. Explanation of the culture model
3. An hour or so on artifacts
4. Focusing on the espoused values
5. Exploration to identify the underlying shared tacit assumptions
6. Exploration of which of these assumptions would help or hinder the evolution of a new way of working in this unit

The meeting was successful in identifying a number of important assumptions. Mary, some of her colleagues on the culture committee, and I all felt that one or more additional groups should be run to flesh out the picture and check our perceptions of what we were hearing. Over the next several months, two more groups were brought together for half-day meetings, leading to a coherent picture of the present corporate culture.

The motivation for defining this picture was that the senior management committee of the unit needed to be involved if new ways of working and values were to be promulgated. Giving them feedback on the culture as we were beginning to see it provided the agenda for a working session with this group. They would elaborate the culture assessment and then make some decisions on what action steps they needed to take to define a new way of working, consistent with their new values.

I decided to give the cultural feedback as much as possible in terms of the language that the assessment groups had used. I also decided at this stage to present "themes" rather than trying to generalize to very abstract concepts, because we wanted the management group to become involved in the assessment process as well and felt that giving them themes would be more concrete. Higher-order generalizations could then be arrived at together during the meeting. Exhibit 4.2 presents the document that was shared with the management group. I commented briefly on each theme during the meeting and encouraged members of the group to comment on how accurate this was in their own experience.

The management group basically bought this picture and confirmed with their own examples that the themes were accurately depicted. This reflection on their own culture allowed the senior management members to think through their own role. They recognized that the most difficult aspect of the Beta culture was the basic fear of being associated with any failure, or of being blamed for anything that went wrong. Furthermore, from the point of view of an engineering culture, they realized how hard it is for engineers to convert themselves into consultants selling themselves and charging clients by the hour.

Exhibit 4.2 Culture Themes Identified in the "Beta Oil" Assessment Workshops

I. Assumptions about the nature of the work to be done

- The organization is energized by identifying problems and developing fixes.
- It works by quick fixes of whatever problems are identified ("fire, ready, aim").
- It is assumed that if you break a problem down into small enough pieces and fix each piece, the big problem gets solved (blindness to interdependencies).
- Problems are recognized and named once variances get high enough. Management then steps in with a quick diagnosis and fix, sets up a new structure or remedial process, and then relaxes and does not follow through on implementation (for example, shortfall on cost recovery).
- We have a "hero" culture: waiting for problems to get serious, then fire fighting and rewarding the successful fire fighters ("But remember, a culture that rewards firefighters breeds arsonists.").
- Quick fixes are always new structures and processes, and once a new structure or process has been put in place the job is done. Implementation is someone else's problem.
- All dilemmas and predicaments are viewed as problems to be solved and are thus subject to the quick structural-fix response. No sensitivity to the complexity of "soft" issues or the difficulties of implementation after a new structure or process is announced.
- Fixes are often the creation of teams or groups, and once a team is formed it is assumed that the job is done (but the culture is basically individualistic; hence teams may not function well).
- Getting involved with implementation is avoided because it exposes you to failure.
- It is assumed that fixes will sell themselves.

Exhibit 4.2 Culture Themes Identified in the "Beta Oil" Assessment Workshops (*continued*)

II. Assumptions about people and their motivation

- It is assumed that people can and will work on their own, that they are highly motivated and dedicated (that is, management does not have to micromanage).
- It is assumed that people will be successful; success is expected and taken for granted.
- It is assumed that people have no ego or social needs on the job.
- You must be willing to sacrifice for the company by working long hours, taking two briefcases home, etc. Nowadays, everyone has two jobs and is expected to be able to do them.
- It is assumed that groups can work on their own and set their own priorities (but there is a sense of lack of direction by management).

III. Assumptions about the management process

- The organization is procedure- and numbers-driven.
- It is all about dollars and costs.
- Surfacing costs is a good thing.
- The organization is numbers-oriented (for example, numerical target for how many people to have in the organization).
- The organization operates with a command-and-control mentality.
- It is assumed that "management decides; others do" (example: when there are jobs to be filled, management just decides who will fill the jobs, with little or no consultation).
- There is very little accountability and great latitude, especially in the intangible or soft areas that are harder to measure.
- Teamwork is espoused but the reward system (forced ranking) is highly individualistic, with emphasis on rewarding "heroes."
- Engineers run the company. You know who is an engineer right away; they are the golden boys who are white, male, tall, clean-cut, and aggressive but not combative.

Exhibit 4.2 Culture Themes Identified in the "Beta Oil" Assessment Workshops (*continued*)

- Company is an autocratic/paternalistic family that takes good care of its children (pays well and has generous—but not portable—retirement) provided they are loyal, hardworking, and successful. If they are somewhat anxious, that is normal and OK.
- A done deal is irreversible.

IV. The organizational "climate"

- Climate is egalitarian, friendly, low-key, and polite, but possibly vicious and blaming when backs are turned.
- We are a punitive, blaming culture.
- You never say you don't know or admit that you made a mistake.
- No one wants to admit to bad things, but people talk about bad things that happened to others.
- When mistakes or failures are identified, blame is assigned quickly and without much systemic analysis; the guilty are named, bad-mouthed, and labeled, which affects their assignments but no formal consequences follow.
- There are not many incentives to work together.
- A single mistake for which you are blamed can offset many successes and result in your being labeled and limited in future assignments and promotions.
- If you are labeled as having made a mistake, it affects whom you can work with in the future, so being negatively labeled can be very destructive to the career.
- Once you are labeled, it is forever; examples are "superior performer," "dinosaur," "not a team player," "high-potential," "low-potential," "not management material."
- Working overtime is the norm.
- Work is done through relationships, and you work with those people whom you know; you use the Old Boy network.

Exhibit 4.2 Culture Themes Identified in the "Beta Oil" Assessment Workshops (*continued*)

- The best strategy for self-protection is building a network of supporters.
- You stay because of the good pay and retirement program (golden handcuffs).
- There is now a climate of fear; the future is uncertain.
- Company used to be a gentle, lifetime employer, but it has had as many as ten rounds of layoffs and downsizings in various divisions.
- As a consequence, there is a real atmosphere of fear, reluctance to confront or complain, avoidance or suppression of conflict.
- Combination of the shift to centralized service with downsizing exacerbates these feelings.
- In a restructuring you can lose scope, rank, or face—but not pay.
- The organization has no obvious supporters.
- Job security is not linked to individual competency.

These insights made it clear that the top priority for the project was to develop a new image of how to work that was consistent with the self-image they had. The culture committee was charged with coming up with a new set of values and practices—the *new way of working*, which would then be promulgated throughout the organization. Whereas in the past "new culture" was thought of as a set of general values such as teamwork, this new way of working was to be *a concrete description based on the culture assessment and the business realities that Beta faced*. The new way of working had to deal with the structural realities of how the engineering job was now defined, but at the same time it had to fit the larger "blaming culture" in which the entire organization was embedded.

To illustrate the power of an assumption like "You must never be associated with any failure because it can be career-threatening," a promising joint venture hit a major snag when it was discovered that the actual project structures would put Beta engineers into situations where they were subordinate to project managers from the other member of the joint venture. The whole planning process unraveled because Beta engineers refused to work for someone from another company. They pointed out that if a project failed, the manager from the other company could simply disappear, while their association with the failure would be negatively viewed within Beta. The fact that the manager was from the other company would not be viewed as a valid excuse.

The impact of the cultural assessment was twofold. It made the senior leaders of the organization aware of the magnitude of the change task they faced, and it made them aware that just announcing a new set of values and goals would not produce the change they desired. Unless they could specify concretely what the new way of working was, they could not expect the engineers in the unit to adapt effectively to the new structural conditions imposed on them.

"Circle Healthcare" Headquarters

This case illustrates how the assessment process reveals some of the critical elements in an organization's subcultures. Note also that we are dealing here with a different kind of organization, a very large health maintenance organization. I was originally called by the HMO's internal OD manager, Robert, to discuss with him some organizational changes that were going to happen. He felt that the Circle culture would be an important factor but was not sure that anyone was paying attention to this element. I functioned as a process consultant (Schein, 1987, 1999), helping Robert decide what kind of intervention would bring awareness of cultural issues to management.

We recognized from the outset that one part of Circle (in terms of historical evolution) was an insurance company driven by typical corporate cultural assumptions, but another part was a doctors' organization run by doctors much more democratically. For example, department chiefs were elected by the other physicians not appointed by senior management. The major question was whether the corporate restructuring would lead to one of these subcultures being taken over, so to speak—or would they blend, or continue to coexist?

In any case, it was important to understand some of the key elements of each subculture. A "diagonal" slice of people representing several ranks from the organization development and human resource departments were brought together to go through the assessment exercise. I followed the same model of explaining the levels of culture and then working from artifacts to values to shared tacit assumptions. However, we added a block of time for the members of the two subgroups to meet to develop their own subculture pictures and to share them with one another.

Following the exercise, which lasted a full day, I took all of the flipcharts and abstracted the key assumptions that surfaced across the entire organization. I inserted parenthetically the editorial comments and questions that occurred to me in my role as the outside consultant. I also appended some "issues and questions," observations about artifacts and observed behavior where the underlying assumptions had not been surfaced (Exhibit 4.3).

This report was mailed to Robert, to be used as he saw fit. Robert and I met several more times over the next few months, but the culture assessment did not lead to any changes in how executive managers moved forward with their own strategy consultants to restructure the organization. They thought the insights were useful but not really relevant to the overall restructuring. I learned later that the "bureaucratic" management subculture of the insurance side of Circle had asserted itself and made changes that were primarily consistent with its own assumptions. The OD function was scaled back and Robert left Circle to become an independent consultant.

Exhibit 4.3 Shared Assumptions in the "Circle Healthcare" Headquarters Organization

I. Key Assumptions

- *We are data-driven*

  We must at all times appear to be data-driven and rational, though "data" are often opinions and/or past experience, not hard data.

- *We are superior*

  We must not look too lavish, and we must always appear humble in public, though we know we are "superior." Many highly paid physicians drive inexpensive cars and in other ways present themselves in public in a more humble fashion. (Is there a need to manage the public image, to present oneself as an organization that watches its costs carefully? Would a physician who displayed wealth be "coached" not to do this?—*E.S.*)

- *We are unique*

  Therefore, we are the only ones who really know what we can and must do. We are the wave of the future. This leads to self-centeredness and indifference to learning from others. (Reliance on consultants, and on having consultants provide alternatives or recommendations rather than struggling with one's own data, is anomalous here and requires further digging; what is the significance of the fact that the group did not want its own data to work with but was willing to let me go off with it and do my own analysis?—*E.S.*)

- *We are hierarchic*

  Decisions are made at the top. (The group asked Michael, their boss, whether another meeting was possible, rather than asserting that they needed to meet again to resolve some of the issues that came up.—*E.S.*).

- *We are bureaucratic*

  We have too much paper and too many signatures to get anything done, and we have an "incapacity to act." (I experienced this in

Exhibit 4.3 Shared Assumptions in the "Circle Healthcare" Headquarters Organization (*continued*)

the group more as a fact to be lived with than a problem to be addressed.—*E.S.*). You don't deal laterally, only through the hierarchy.

- *We have two strong subcultures*

  They coexist in a complex symbiosis (my word—*E.S.*). First is the physician subculture, which is organizationally a professional partnership (a layered hierarchy—*E.S.*) consisting of many specialties and short career ladders. Second is a managerial bureaucratic subculture in which work, pay, status, and career lines are defined by rising in the hierarchy. In the professional subculture, one can move up into management and back down into one's specialty; in the managerial subculture one can only move up. In the professional subculture, employees can earn more than their managers, that is, physicians-in-chief; in the managerial one, the managers must always earn more than their subordinates. For example, a nursing supervisor renegotiated the contract with the nurses union when she discovered that some nurses were making more than she was.

  Status is clearly associated with being a physician, and only they are called professionals. The other functions are support and ancillary. Rage toward physicians is publicly suppressed, but physician bashing is a fine art. Physicians are a sacred cow, but paradoxically they feel quite powerless. They are often the most stable group in the system in terms of turnover.

- *We are action oriented*

  Whatever is worth doing can and should be done quickly. Important things should not take too long. (Is the reverse true? If it cannot be done quickly, it is not worth doing? That is, if we cannot decipher our culture in a few hours then let's forget about that task, or let someone else worry about it and bring back some "answers."—*E.S.*)

Exhibit 4.3 Shared Assumptions in the "Circle Healthcare" Headquarters Organization (*continued*)

II. Additional Observations

The next few points are observations made by the group, but the assumptions behind them are not clear and we did not have time to explore them.

- There are tensions between headquarters ("region") and facilities (medical centers), especially around the feeling that the centers have cut costs while region continues to live high off the hog. Regional is seen as having cushier facilities, getting more money relative to the centers, always asking for more than they need. There is no cost accounting and no performance measurement.
- People come to meetings late, walk in and out, and leave when they feel like it (this happened in our meeting.—*E.S.*).
- There is always food (is this a reflection of a nurturing paternalism?—*E.S.*).
- We value commitment and loyalty to the organization.
- There is a strong sense of a Protestant work ethic. The more work you do, the more work you get. Time for reflection or thinking is not sanctioned.
- Dress is generally informal, but at casual functions nurses dress up more.
- Physician salaries are officially secret and to be kept so.
- Education and training are highly available and highly valued.
- You cannot get fired, except for stealing or possibly breaking confidences.
- Satisfactory ratings are provided even for marginal employees; there is very little negative feedback, and also few rewards for quality performance. Good attendance and longevity are valued, not long hours. Long hours only get you more work.
- There are lots of meetings, and political consensus is built up there. Lots of use of e-mail, phones, fax.

Exhibit 4.3 Shared Assumptions in the "Circle Healthcare" Headquarters Organization (*continued*)

III. Issues and Questions

- Is the "incapacity to act" a reflection of bureaucratic barriers, or complacency based on some deep level of self-satisfaction and feeling of superiority and invulnerability?
- How much of the above description is a function of the subculture of organization development (and not reflective of the "Circle Healthcare" culture)?
- Where are the forces toward the desired strategic changes of innovation, cost reduction, and more employee involvement? (The only place I see it is in the physician subculture, which is based more on partnership than managerial or bureaucratic principles.—*E.S.*)
- How can a dialogue be created that permits deciphering the best elements of each subculture so that the future can be built on a set of assumptions that represents an optimum integration of the professional and hierarchical subcultures? This process must begin with valuing both subcultures based upon the insight that both have some elements that are functional, but also some that are dysfunctional. That is, how do you reduce costs and remain affordable without compromising the quantity and quality of health care? The danger is that the managerial subculture will attempt to overwhelm the physician subculture, and this will lead either to paralysis because of resistance on the part of the physicians or a cutback in quantity and quality of health care.

The "Delta" Sales Organization

Delta is the U.S. subsidiary of a large European pharmaceutical company. The vice president of sales had been in his job for thirty years and was widely credited with having built up a very successful sales organization. The culture issue came up around the question of whether to replace him afer his retirement with an inside candidate, thereby reinforcing the culture that had been built over a long time, or bringing in an outsider, thereby setting in motion cultural changes toward another type of sales organization. In this case, the goal of the assessment was not only to understand the present culture of the sales organization but also to evaluate it to see whether it should be perpetuated or changed.

I met with the top executive team and determined that they were indeed open to either alternative. What they wanted was an effective sales organization; they would measure this effectiveness by determining first of all how they felt about the culture we would uncover, and second, how the members of the sales organization felt about their own culture. The basic assessment plan was for me to work my way down through the organization, doing individual or group interviews as seemed appropriate.

During our planning process, an important issue came up. The current VP of sales expected me to do extensive individual interviews to decipher the culture. I had to convince him that it was not only more valid but far more efficient to work with groups, unless there was reason to believe that group members would be inhibited in talking about the culture in front of others. The result was that I interviewed individuals at the top level of the organization, where inhibition might operate; but as I got to the regional and district organizations I ran group meetings along the lines described above.

Exhibit 4.4 gives some excerpts from my report, which led eventually to appointment of the inside candidate and reflected the decision to preserve and reinforce the existing culture. Notice that in this case the artifacts and values are more salient and the tacit assumptions are implied but not made explicit.

Exhibit 4.4 Excerpts from the "Delta" Sales Culture Report

- There is a very strong sales culture that was largely created over the last several decades by the present vice president, who is about to retire.
- This sales culture is credited with being the reason why the company has been as successful as it is.
- The present sales culture is perceived to be the company's best hope for the future. The sales organization feels strongly that it should not be tampered with.
- The key elements of the sales culture—its strengths—are:
  1. The high morale, dedication, and loyalty of the sales reps
  2. The high degree of flexibility of the reps in responding to changing management demands in marketing existing products
  3. The high degree of openness of communication, which permits rapid problem solving, collaboration, and shifting of strategy when needed
  4. Good communication and collaboration between district managers and reps
  5. A strong family feeling, informal relationships up and down the hierarchy; everyone is known to management on a first-name basis and employees trust management
  6. There is a strong development program that gives sales reps multiple career options according to their talents and needs
  7. High ethical and professional standards in selling; focus on educating doctors, not just pushing individual products
  8. High degree of discipline in following company directives in how to position products; feeling that "management showed us how to do it, and it worked"
- There was a strong feeling that only an insider would understand the culture they had built. Bringing in an outsider would be very risky

Exhibit 4.4 Excerpts from the "Delta" Sales Culture Report (*continued*)

because he or she might undermine or destroy the very things they felt made them effective.

- Though the culture is authoritarian and hierarchic, it works very well because top management gets across the message that it is the reps and the districts who make the system go, and that what management is doing is in support of the front lines. It is a very people-oriented culture that allows for both flexibility and discipline. For example, every district follows the sales and marketing plan, but every district manager allows the reps to use their own skills and biases to their own best advantage and does not impose arbitrary methods to be used in every case. Reps feel they have some autonomy but feel obligated and committed to company plans.
- The individual and group incentive and bonus systems are working well in keeping an optimum balance between individual competition and teamwork. The management system is very sensitive to the need to balance these forces, and it does so at the higher level as well between the sales and marketing organizations.
- The wider company culture is very people-oriented and makes multiple career paths available. The emphasis on personal growth and development, supplemented by thorough training, emanates from the top of the company and is perceived as the reason why people are so motivated.

The report illustrates how a culture assessment can be used to deal with a very specific question—in this case, a decision on senior management succession. If there had been more conflict or discord in the culture, the decision would have been more complex, but, as it turned out, throughout the organization there was unanimity that the present culture was well adapted to the business situation and should therefore be preserved and enhanced.

Naval Research Labs

The fourth and last case illustrates how the decision to assess the culture of an organization because of presumed geographic subculture issues led to a completely unexpected set of insights about other subcultural dynamics that were operating.

The initial goal was to determine how the geographical and structural differences between the Naval Research Lab unit that was located in New England and its administrative-political unit in Washington, D.C., might have created subcultures. The two units had different populations and tasks, so it was anticipated that there would be important subcultural differences that would create communication problems.

I was contacted by an MIT alumnus who worked in the labs and knew about my work on culture. He introduced me to senior management, and we decided to create a one-day assessment workshop in which we would explore the geographic subcultures, using my methodology. The assessment was done by senior managers representing both the research and administrative units. As we proceeded, it was revealed that an important set of structural differences not previously noticed had to be taken into account. The Naval Research Labs worked in terms of projects, and each project had particular financial sponsorship. Therefore, every project had its own administrative staff working in Washington to develop budgets, keep sponsors informed, and generally manage all of the external political issues that might come up.

What was originally perceived as two units, one in Washington and one in New England, turned out to be *nine*—each of which had both a New England and Washington subunit! However, because it was so critical for each project to work smoothly, the geographic factor was overcome in all nine projects, through multiple meetings and constant communication. Each project thus developed a subculture based on the nature of its work and its people, and there were indeed subcultural differences among the projects. But the original notion that there was a geographic problem had to be dropped completely.

The important learning from this exercise was that the focus on culture revealed some structures in the organization that had not really been thought significant before. Where geographic separation mattered, each project had already done a great deal to ameliorate the potential negative consequences. As in the Delta case, the assessment revealed that the subcultures should be preserved rather than changed.

The Bottom Line

I have tried in this chapter to convince you of several things:

- Culture *can* be assessed by means of individual and group interview processes, with group interviews being by far the better method both in terms of validity and efficiency. Such assessments can be usefully made in as little as half a day.
- Culture *cannot* be assessed by means of surveys or questionnaires because one does not know what to ask and cannot judge the reliability and validity of the responses. Survey responses can be viewed as cultural artifacts and as reflections of the organization's climate, but they do not say anything about the deeper values or shared assumptions that are operating.
- A culture assessment is of little value unless it is tied to some organizational problem or issue. In other words, diagnosing a culture for its own sake is not only too vast a problem but also may be viewed as boring and useless. On the other hand, if the organization has a purpose, a new strategy, or a problem to be solved, then to determine how the culture impacts the issue is not only useful but in most cases necessary. The issue should be related to the organization's effectiveness and stated as concretely as possible. One cannot say that "the culture" is an issue or problem. The culture has an impact on how the organization performs, and the focus should initially be on where performance needs to be improved.

- The assessment process should first identify cultural assumptions and then assess them in terms of whether they are strengths or constraints on what the organization is trying to do. In most organizational change efforts, it is much easier to draw on the strengths of the culture than to overcome the constraints by changing the culture.
- In any cultural assessment process, one should be sensitive to the presence of subcultures and prepared to do separate assessments of them to determine their relevance to what the organization is trying to do.
- Culture can be described and assessed at the levels of artifacts, espoused values, and shared tacit assumptions. The importance of getting to the assumption level derives from the insight that unless you understand the shared tacit assumptions, you cannot explain the discrepancies that almost always surface between espoused values and observed behavioral artifacts.

Now that you understand something of the process of cultural assessment, you are ready to think about how to build, evolve, enhance, or maybe even change culture.

Part Two

Corporate Culture in Action

Chapter Five

Culture Creation, Evolution, and Change in Start-Up Companies

- Founding and Early Growth
- How Founders and Leaders Embed Cultural Elements
- Culture Change Mechanism
- The Impact of Size and the Loss of "Functional Familiarity": From Personal Management to Contracts, Systems, and Processes
- Managing Problems of Succession
- The Bottom Line

The nature of culture change depends upon what stage of growth an organization is in. In this and the next three chapters, I will describe these processes and show you what is involved if you want to manage them in the process of founding and growth; in midlife in the still-successful organization; in the mature and declining organization; and in mergers, acquisitions, and various kinds of joint ventures.

Founding and Early Growth

The most salient cultural characteristic of young organizations is that they are the creation of founders and founding families. The personal beliefs, assumptions, and values of the entrepreneur or founder are imposed on the people he or she hires, and—if the organization is successful—they come to be shared, seen as correct, and eventually taken for granted. The shared beliefs, assumptions, and values then function in the organization as the basic glue that holds it together, the major source of the organization's sense of identity, and the major way of defining its distinctive competence. At this stage, culture is the organization's primary asset, but it is repeatedly tested by being acted out. If it is reinforced, if the organization succeeds, the culture grows stronger. If the organization fails, the founders are likely to be thrown out and their assumptions come to be challenged and probably abandoned.

Case Example: "Jones Food"

Founder Harold Jones was an immigrant whose parents had started a corner grocery store in a large urban area in the 1930s. His parents, particularly his mother, taught him some basic attitudes toward customers and helped him form the vision that he could succeed in building a successful enterprise. He assumed from the beginning that if he did things right he would succeed and build a major organization that would bring him and his family a fortune. Ultimately, he built a large chain of supermarkets, department stores, and related businesses that dominated its market area for many decades.

Jones was the major ideological force in his company throughout its history and continued to impose his assumptions on the company until his death in his late seventies. He assumed that his primary mission was to supply a high-quality, reliable product to customers in clean, attractive surroundings. His customers' needs were the primary consideration in all major decisions. There are many stories about how Jones, as a young man operating the corner grocery store with his wife, gave customers credit and thus displayed trust in them. He always took products back if there was the slightest complaint, and he kept his store absolutely spotless to inspire customer confidence in his products. Each of these mandates later became a major policy in his chain of stores and was taught and reinforced by close personal supervision.

Jones believed that only personal example and close supervision would ensure subordinates' adequate performance. He would show up at his stores unexpectedly, inspect even minor details, and then—by personal example, by stories of how other stores were solving the problems identified, by articulating rules, and by exhortation—"teach" the staff what they should be doing. He often lost his temper and berated subordinates who did not follow the rules or principles that he laid down.

Jones expected his store managers to be highly visible, be very much on top of their own jobs, and supervise closely in the same way he did, reflecting deep assumptions about the nature of good management. These assumptions became a major theme in later years in his concept of "visible management," the assumption that a "good" manager always had to be around to set an example and teach subordinates the right way to do things.

The founding group in this company consisted essentially of Harold's three brothers. But one "lieutenant" who was not a family member was recruited early; along with the founder, he became the main culture creator and carrier. Sharing Jones's basic assumptions about how to run a business, he set up formal systems to ensure that those assumptions became the basis for operating realities. After Jones's death, this lieutenant continued to articulate the theory of visible management and tried to set a personal example of how to do it by continuing the same close supervisory policies that Jones had used.

One of Jones's assumptions was that one could win in the marketplace only by being highly innovative and technically on the forefront. He always encouraged his managers to try new approaches, brought in a variety of consultants who advocated new approaches to human resource management, started selection and development programs through assessment centers long before other companies tried this approach, and traveled to conventions and other businesses where new technological innovations were displayed, resulting in his company being one of the first to introduce barcode technology. He was always willing to experiment to improve the business. Jones's view of truth and reality was that one had to find it wherever one could, and therefore it was important to be open to the environment and never take it for granted that one had all the answers.

If things worked, Jones encouraged their adoption; if they did not, he ordered them dropped. Measuring results and solving problems were for him intensely personal matters, deriving from his theory of visible management. In addition to using a variety of traditional business measures, he always made it a point to visit all his stores personally; if he saw things not to his liking, he corrected them immediately and decisively even if it meant someone had to go around the authority chain. He trusted only those managers who operated by assumptions similar to his own, and he clearly had favorites to whom he delegated more authority.

Power and authority in this organization remained very centralized, in that everyone knew Jones or his chief lieutenant could—and would—override decisions made by division or unit managers without consultation, and often peremptorily. The ultimate source of power—the voting shares of stock—were owned entirely by Jones and his wife, so that after his death his wife was in total control of the company.

Jones was interested in developing good managers throughout the organization, but he never assumed that sharing ownership through granting stock options would contribute to that process. He paid his key managers very well but did not share ownership even with those who had been with the company throughout its history. In this area, the assumption was that ownership was strictly a family matter, to the point that he was not even willing to share stock with the man who was his chief lieutenant, close friend, and virtual cobuilder of the company.

Jones placed several family members in key managerial positions and gave them favored treatment in the form of good developmental jobs that would test them early for ultimate management potential. As the firm diversified, family members were made division heads, even though they often had relatively little management experience. If a family member performed poorly, he would be bolstered by having a good manager introduced under him; if the operation then improved, the relative would likely be given the credit. If things continued badly, the family member would be moved out, though with various face-saving excuses.

My introduction to the company concerned this dynamic. Jones had only daughters and had moved the husband of his oldest daughter into the presidency of his company. This man was a very congenial person but not trained for his general management position, so Jones authorized the creation of a management development program for the top twenty-five people in the organization (the hidden agenda was to teach his son-in-law something about management). Jones's chief lieutenant brought me in as a consultant and trainer in the program; I was told from the outset that part of the goal was to educate the son-in-law.

Peer relationships among nonfamily members inevitably became highly politicized. They were officially defined as "competitive"; Jones believed firmly in the value of interpersonal competition. Winners would be rewarded and losers discarded. However, since family members were in positions of power, one had to know how to stay on the good side of those family members without losing the trust of peers, on whom one was dependent.

Jones wanted open communication and a high level of trust among all members of the organization, but his own assumptions about the role of the family and the correct way to manage were, to a large degree, in conflict with each other. Many members of the organization banded together in a kind of mutual protection society, which developed a culture of its own. They were more loyal to each other than to the company and had a high rate of interaction, which bred assumptions and norms that became to some degree countercultural to the founder's.

Several things should be noted at this point. By definition, something becomes part of the culture only if it works, in the sense of making the organization successful and reducing the anxiety of the members (including Jones). His assumptions about how things should be done were congruent with the kind of environment in which he operated, so he and the founding group received strong reinforcement for those assumptions. As the company grew and prospered, Jones perceived more and more confirmation of his assumptions and thus felt confident that they were correct. Throughout his lifetime, he steadfastly adhered to those assumptions and did everything in his power to get others to accept them. However, as has been noted, some of the assumptions made nonfamily managers more anxious, thus leading to the formation of a counterculture.

Jones also learned that he had to share some concepts and assumptions with a great many other people. As the company grew and learned from its own experience, his assumptions gradually had to be modified in some areas. If not, he had to withdraw from active management of those areas. For example, in its diversification efforts, the company bought several production units that would enable it to integrate vertically in certain food and clothing lines where it was economically advantageous to do so. But when Jones learned that he knew relatively little about production, he brought in strong managers and gave them a great deal of autonomy. Some of the production divisions never acquired the culture of the main organization, and the heads of those divisions never enjoyed the status and security that insiders had.

Eventually, the founder also learned somewhat painfully that he did not send the clear and consistent signals he thought he did. Unable to perceive his own conflicts and inconsistencies, he could not understand why some of his best young managers failed to respond to his competitive incentives and even left the company. He thought he was adequately motivating them and could not see that for some of them the political climate, absence of stock options, and arbitrary rewarding of family members made their own career progress too uncertain. Jones was perplexed and angry about much of this, blaming the young managers while clinging to his assumptions and conflicts.

Following his death, the company experienced a long period of cultural turmoil because of the vacuum created by Jones's absence and the retirement of several other key culture carriers.

But the basic philosophies of how to run stores were thoroughly embedded and remained. Various family members continued to run the company, though none of them possessed the business skills that Jones had.

With the retirement of the chief lieutenant, a period of instability set in, marked by the discovery that some of the managers who had been cultivated under Jones were not as strong and capable as had been assumed. None of his children or their spouses were able to take over the business decisively, so an outsider was brought in to run the company. This person predictably failed because he could not adapt to the culture and to the family.

After two more failures with CEOs drawn from other companies, the family turned to a manager who had originally been with Jones Food and subsequently made a fortune elsewhere in real estate enterprises. This manager stabilized the business because he had more credibility by virtue of his prior history and his knowledge of how to handle family members. Under his leadership, some of the original assumptions began to evolve in new directions. Eventually the family decided to sell the Jones company, and this manager and one of the cousins started a business of their own, which ended up competing with Jones Food.

One clear lesson from the Jones Food case is that a culture does not survive if the main culture carriers depart and if most members of the organization are to some degree conflicted because of the mixed messages from the leaders during the growth period. Jones Food had a strong culture, but the founder's own conflicts became embedded in that culture, creating conflict and ultimately lack of stability.

How Founders and Leaders Embed Cultural Elements

How founders and leaders create and embed culture can be summarized by looking at the various mechanisms described in Exhibit 5.1.

By far, the most important of these mechanisms is the leader's own behavior. When it comes to culture creation and embedding,

Exhibit 5.1 How Leaders Embed Cultural Elements

I. Primary embedding mechanisms

- What leaders pay attention to, measure, and control regularly
- How leaders react to critical incidents and organizational crises
- Observed criteria by which leaders allocate scarce resources
- Deliberate role modeling, teaching, and coaching
- Observed criteria by which leaders allocate rewards and status
- Observed criteria by which leaders recruit, select, promote, retire, and excommunicate organizational members

II. Secondary articulation and reinforcement mechanisms

- Organization design and structure
- Organizational systems and procedures
- Organizational rites and rituals
- Design of physical space, façades, and buildings
- Stories, legends, and myths about people and events
- Formal statements of organizational philosophy, values, and creed

"walking the talk" has special significance in that new members pay far more attention to the walk than the talk. Especially important is what the leader attends to, measures, gets upset about, rewards, and punishes. The supporting mechanisms of structures and processes become more important in the organization's midlife, as new generations of leaders are heavily influenced by these structures and processes. In extreme cases, these elements even determine what kind of person is accepted as the leader. But in a young and growing organization, the personal behavior of the leader is by far the most important determinant of how the culture is shaped.

Culture Change Mechanisms

The members of a young successful company cling to their assumptions for two reasons. First, the assumptions are their own invention and a product of their own experience. Second, they reflect the values of the founder(s) or founding family, who still have the power that comes from ownership. If the founders say, "This is the way we will do it, and this is what I believe," then members jeopardize their careers if they say there is a better way that ought to be tried. If the organization is succeeding, they feel disrespectful to be challenging the beliefs of the father figures. In other words, this kind of evolving culture is very strongly held.

The emphasis in this early stage is on differentiating oneself from the environment and from other organizations. The organization makes its culture explicit, integrates it as much as possible, and teaches it firmly to newcomers (or selects them for reasons of initial compatibility). One also sees in young companies a bias toward certain business functions, which influences the kind of culture that arises. In Jones Food, there was a distinct bias toward retailing and customers, whereas in DEC the bias was clearly toward engineering and manufacturing. Not only was it difficult for Digital's other functions to acquire status and prestige, but professionals such as marketers were often told by managers who had been with the company from its origin that "marketers never know what they are talking about." In Ciba-Geigy, the early bias toward science and research remained even though the company was much older. Since R&D was historically the basis of the company's success, science was defined as the distinctive competence, even though more and more managers admitted overtly that the future hinged on marketing, tight financial controls, and efficient operations.

The implications for change at this stage are clear. The culture in young and successfully growing companies is likely to be very strongly adhered to because:

- The primary culture creators are still present
- The culture helps the organization define itself and make its way into a potentially hostile environment
- Many elements of the culture have been learned as defenses against anxiety as the organization struggles to build and maintain itself

Proposals to *deliberately change* the culture, whether from inside or outside, are therefore likely to be totally ignored or resisted. Instead, dominant members or coalitions attempt to preserve and enhance the culture. The only force that might unfreeze such a situation is an external crisis of survival, in the form of a sharp drop in growth rate, loss of sales or profit, a major product failure, or some other event that cannot be ignored (Dyer, 1986). If such a crisis occurs, a transition to the next stage (being managed by an outsider) may automatically be launched. The crisis may discredit the founder and bring a new senior manager into the picture. If the founding organization itself stays intact, so does the culture. How, then, does culture evolve in the growth phase of an organization? Which processes can be actively managed, from the perspective of either a leader or a consultant?

Several change processes can be identified.

Incremental Change Through General and Specific Evolution

If the organization continues to be successful and if the founder or founding family is around for a long time, the culture evolves in small increments by continuing to assimilate what works best over the years. *General* evolution involves diversification, growing complexity, higher levels of differentiation and integration, and creative synthesis into new and higher forms. *Specific* evolution involves adapting specific parts of the organization to their particular environments, thus creating subcultures that eventually have an impact on the core culture. These mechanisms cause organizations within varied industries to develop distinct industry cultures. Thus, a high-technology company develops highly refined R&D skills, while a consumer products company in foods or cosmetics develops highly refined marketing skills.

In each case, such differences reflect important underlying assumptions about the nature of the world and the actual growth experience of the organization. In addition, since the parts of the organization exist in different environments, each part evolves to adapt to its particular environment. As subgroups differentiate and subcultures develop, opportunities for major culture change arise, but in this stage they are only tolerated and efforts are made to minimize them. These evolutionary processes happen whether you do anything specific or not, but if you become aware of the processes you can aid them by imparting insight.

Practical Implication

If you do not see any pressing business problems in how things are going, just observe and roll with the punches. If you see problems, start a process of developing insight, based on these culture dynamics.

Guiding Evolution Through Fostering Insight

If you think of culture as a mechanism for making the world meaningful and predictable, for avoiding the anxiety that comes with unpredictability and meaninglessness, you can help members of the organization by making explicit the cultural themes and elements. If you gain insight into what your shared assumptions are and why you hold on to them, there is a better chance of evaluating them to determine how functional they continue to be as the environment around you changes. The internal deciphering process described in Chapter Four typically has the effect of producing a level of cultural insight that allows a group to decide the direction of its future evolution. The key roles of the leader in this process are to recognize the need for such an intervention and to manage the internal assessment process. Though leaders would not typically describe this as therapy, it is functionally the equivalent, for groups, of what individuals undergo when they seek therapeutic help because things are not working. The key role of the consultant in this process is to activate leadership to become supportive of such insight-producing activities.

An example of change through sudden insight occurred in "Gamma Tech," a company that had always lived by the assumption that marketing was a useless function relative to others, yet its survival increasingly depended upon effective marketing. In assessing their own culture, senior managers discovered that they shared a very limited definition of marketing, as just "merchandising the products we already have." With the help of an outside consultant, managers gained the insight that their definition of marketing was biased and limited. They were then able through educating themselves to redefine in their own mind that marketing included building up Gamma Tech's company image, improving the connection between customers and the product development functions, training the field salesforce on the characteristics of the new products, developing a long-range product strategy, and integrating various product lines according to projections of where future customer needs would be.

Gamma Tech's managers suddenly realized that all of the specific things they needed to do better were, in fact, marketing. They began to see in their marketing managers skills they had not observed before, and this permitted them to begin valuing their marketing peers and moving them into more central roles in the management process. From an assumption that marketing was useless, they moved to a belief that marketing might be highly valuable, by redefining in their mind what marketing was. As they paid attention to various marketing functions, success came—and they gradually adopted the assumption that marketing was crucial to their continued existence.

Many of the interventions that have occurred over the years in DEC can be seen as therapeutic in that the goal was insight. For example, at one annual corporate seminar of the top eighty managers the company's poor performance was being discussed. A depressive mood overtook them and was finally articulated: "We could do better, if only our president or one of his key lieutenants would decide on a direction and tell us which way to go."

Those of us familiar with the culture heard this not as a realistic request but as a wish for a magic solution. I was scheduled to give a short presentation on the company's culture and used the opportunity to raise a question: "Given the history of this company and the kinds of managers and people that you are, if Ken Olsen marched in here right now and told everyone in what directions he wanted you to go, do you think you would follow?" There was a long silence and then gradually a few knowing smiles. A more realistic discussion ensued. The group collectively realized that, given their history, they would not accept orders from above anyway—even from Olsen—and that they had better get busy to work out for themselves a new sense of direction. In effect, the group reaffirmed and strengthened its assumptions about individual responsibility and autonomy, but these senior managers also recognized that their wish for marching orders was really a wish for more discipline in the organization—and that this discipline could be achieved among themselves by tighter coordination at their own level.

Dysfunctional assumptions do not always have to be given up. Sometimes it is enough to recognize how they operate, so that their consequences can be realistically assessed. If the consequences are considered too costly, one can engage in compensatory behavior. For example, DEC's commitment to checking all decisions laterally before moving ahead (even though this slowed things down) was affirmation of the assumption that one could only test the ultimate correctness of a decision by getting broad buy-in. If this becomes too dysfunctional, one can (1) design compensatory mechanisms (for example, have less frequent but longer meetings, or classify decisions and seek consensus only on certain ones, or find ways to speed up meetings) or (2) break the company down into smaller units in which the consensual process can work because people know each other.

Practical Implications

If the result of insight is that the organization chooses to reaffirm its culture, several concrete mechanisms can be used to ensure continuity:

- Be certain that new hires fit the cultural mold.
- Identify and reward behavior consistent with cultural assumptions.
- Identify and punish behavior that violates important assumptions and values.
- Create or perpetuate training, socialization, indoctrination, and mentoring programs that bring newcomers into contact with old-timers.

If, on the other hand, insight produces the realization that the culture must evolve in new directions, then you have to intervene along the lines discussed in the next sections.

Managed Evolution Through Promotion of "Hybrids"

Changes in the environment often create disequilibria that force real change. How can a young organization so highly committed to its identity make such changes? One mechanism is a process of gradual and incremental change through systematic promotion of insiders whose own assumptions are better adapted to the new external realities. Because they are insiders, they accept much of the cultural core and have credibility. But, because of their personalities or life experiences, or the subculture in which their careers developed, they hold assumptions that are in varying degrees different from those at the core and thus can move the organization gradually into new ways of thinking and acting. If such managers are put into key positions, they often elicit a feeling from others on the order of "We don't like what she is doing in the way of changing the place, but at least she is one of us."

For this mechanism to work, some of the company's most senior leaders must have insight into what is missing. This implies that they must first become *marginal enough in their own organization* to be able to perceive their corporate culture accurately. They may obtain such insight through the questions of board members, from consultants, or through educational programs where they meet other leaders. If the leaders then recognize the need for change, they can begin to select for key jobs those members of the existing culture who best represent the new assumptions they want to enhance.

For example, at one stage in its history DEC found itself rapidly losing the ability to coordinate the efforts of large numbers of units. Olsen and other senior managers knew that bringing an outsider into a key position would be rejected, so they attempted to gradually fill several key positions with managers who had grown up in manufacturing and in field service, where discipline and centralization had been the norm. These managers operated within the culture but gradually tried to impose more centralization and discipline.

Similarly, once Ciba-Geigy recognized the need to become more marketing-oriented, it began to appoint to senior positions managers who had grown up in the pharmaceutical division where the importance of marketing had been recognized earlier.

Organizations sometimes attempt to achieve such changes by bringing in outsiders, but at this stage the culture is too strong and they either come to adopt it or fail and are ejected. As we shall see, at a later stage outsiders play a bigger role. On the other hand, with the growth of subcultures, finding "hybrids" within the organization becomes more feasible, as we discuss next.

Practical Implication

Identify and promote into key positions individuals who accept the core strengths of the culture but who have other values and assumptions more in line with where you feel the organization needs to go. Try to locate such individuals within the organization so that they are accepted as members of the existing culture.

Taking Advantage of the Growth of Subcultures

If the founder's beliefs are well adapted to the environmental realities the new organization faces, it grows and ages. With growth and aging come several new organizational phenomena. Strong subunits arise based on function, geography, markets, or products, and these subunits have to survive in their various external environments. Thus, in adapting to these external environments they evolve beliefs and assumptions that are congruent with but different from the core assumptions of the founder. Such subcultures are often called silos or stove pipes if they reflect functions, products, markets, or geographies. The boundaries they build around themselves make it harder to communicate across them and integrate their various efforts.

But this is not the only kind of subculture that forms. With age, each set of employees and managers *at a given level within the organization* also shares common experiences that become the basis for mutually held assumptions about how things are and how they should be done. The shared assumptions of employees differ from those of management, especially if workers are unionized and particularly so if they belong to an international union. First-line supervisors develop shared assumptions based on the nature of their jobs. Staff groups such as engineering, finance, and planning develop their own, based on their professional and occupational backgrounds. Middle managers develop subcultures based on the similarities of their roles. Perhaps most important of all, so do CEOs and the people they take into their confidence, sharing assumptions regarding the financial concerns of their organizations.

It is especially crucial to understand some subcultures, especially engineering and top management, because the reference group—the group to which members compare themselves—lies outside the organization in the occupational community (Schein, 1996; Van Maanen and Barley, 1984). Thus, for engineers and other organizational designers it is the design profession that dictates many of the values and assumptions they live by. They are likely to share assumptions that perfect designs are free of people and that it is people who make mistakes and should be engineered out of processes as much as possible. The subculture of engineering and design, then, is potentially in conflict with various operator, line, and sales units that depend on people and teamwork for effective performance.

In the case of CEOs it is their board, the financial markets, the analyst community, and fellow CEOs in the industry that define the environment and thereby create some of the assumptions that CEOs learn to live by. However much they believe that people are important, their job demands primary attention to the financial affairs of the organization; inevitably, people come to be seen as a cost factor. In practice, the CEO subculture is also out of sync with the engineering subculture because of the latter's desire to build the most elegant system, which is usually too costly. Hence the degree to which these occupational subcultures are aligned with each other is a major determinant of how well the organization as a whole functions. Your role as a culture leader might well be to ensure that these subcultures are accepted as necessary and needing alignment. It does not help the organization if each subculture believes the others are dysfunctional. Your job as a culture change agent is to develop meetings and events where mutual understanding can arise among them.

Practical Implications

- Create assessment processes to identify the assumptions of various subcultures, by function, product line, market, geography, occupational community, and echelon.
- Examine dysfunctional stereotyping across these cultural boundaries.
- Create events that permit communication and dialogue to improve mutual understanding and alignment of subcultures.
- If some subcultures represent assumptions and values more in line with environmental requirements, promote people from the subcultures into key organizational positions.

The Impact of Size and the Loss of "Functional Familiarity": From Personal Management to Contracts, Systems, and Processes

When differentiation into various kinds of subcultures occurs in a small organization where everyone knows everyone else, the communication difficulties that might arise during coordination efforts can be resolved informally. People are "functionally familiar" with each other in that they know one another's working styles, what verbal commitments mean, the time horizons that are used, and generally how to calibrate each other. With growth in organizational size, people can no longer remain functionally familiar with others, so they have to resort to more formal processes of contracting, monitoring each other, and in general substituting processes and procedures for personal contact.

To revisit this concept, when DEC was small a hardware engineer could go to the software department and ask whether the supporting software would be ready in six months so that the product could be launched. The software manager would say "Sure." The hardware manager would then tell me that he "knew" that this meant nine months because "he is always a bit optimistic but he will get it done, so I can plan accordingly." As DEC became large and more differentiated, the same scenario would no longer produce the same result. The software manager would again say "Sure," but the hardware manager would tell me that he was unsure whether that meant six months, nine months, twelve months, or never, because some other priorities might bump his project. The software manager was now a stranger, embedded in other organizations, someone with an unknown personality. The hardware manager now had to resort to getting a written commitment so that he could hold the software manager to it. Bureaucracy was born.

As deals have to be negotiated with strangers, trust levels erode, and political processes begin to replace teamwork in pursuit of common goals. The subunits become power centers, and their leaders become barons with an increasingly local agenda. Echelons of supervision, midlevel, and senior management develop their own norms and force the communications going up and down the hierarchy into certain forms. As examples, engineers learn that they have to put their design ideas into cost-benefit language to get middle management to look at proposals, and middle management learns that it has to show the benefits of the project in terms of the particular financial issues the CEO is grappling with at the time (Thomas, 1994).

For as long as the founders or founding families retain ownership and control, they can function as the integrating force and use some of the basic assumptions of the culture as the primary integrating and control mechanism. Charismatic founder-owners can continue to be the glue by articulating the values and principles they expect organization management to follow. But, with continuing success, the impact of size and age makes this form of coordination harder to implement. The inability of founders to let go increases the danger that dysfunctional elements of the culture will be perpetuated, and that new managers with adaptively appropriate assumptions and values will not be permitted to gain power. How succession is managed then becomes a major issue.

Practical Implications

- Watch for symptoms of loss of functional familiarity: Misunderstanding across subcultural boundaries, loss of trust, and growth of formal contracting and other bureaucratic processes.
- Create events (meetings, special projects, joint travel, social occasions) that rebuild functional familiarity, that allow people who must work together to get to know each other personally.

Managing Problems of Succession

Succession from founders and owning families to midlife under general managers involves a number of subphases and processes. How companies actually move from being under the domination of a founder or family to the state of being managed by second-, third-, and fourth-generation general managers has so many variants that one can only identify some prototypical processes and events.

The first—and often most critical—of these processes is the shift from the founder to the next CEO, whether a family member or an outsider. Even if this person is the founder's son, daughter, or other trusted family member, it is in the nature of founder-entrepreneurs to have difficulty giving up what they have created. In extreme cases, a founder may be unconsciously willing even to destroy his organization to prove to the world how indispensable he was. On the other hand, some entrepreneurs whose passion is to keep creating new ventures find it easy to go public and step down or turn successful ventures over to friends and colleagues.

During the transition phase, conflict over which elements of the culture employees like or do not like reflects what they do or do not like about the founder, since most of the culture is likely to be a playing out of the founder's personality. Battles develop between "conservatives," who like the founding culture, and "liberals" or "radicals," who want to change the culture (partly because they want to enhance their own power position). The danger in this situation is that feelings about the founder are projected onto the culture, and in the effort to displace the leader much of the culture comes under challenge. If members of the organization forget that the culture is a set of learned solutions that have produced success, comfort, and identity, then they may try to change the very things they value and need.

Often missing in this phase is understanding of what the culture is and what it is doing for the organization, regardless of how it came to be. Succession processes must therefore be designed to enhance those parts of the culture that provide identity, distinctive competence, and protection from anxiety. Such a process can probably be managed only from within, because an outsider could not possibly understand the subtleties of the cultural issues and the emotional relationships between founders and employees.

Preparation for succession is usually psychologically difficult both for the founder and for potential successors because entrepreneurs typically like to maintain a high level of control. They may officially be grooming successors, but unconsciously they may be preventing powerful and competent people from functioning in these roles. Or they may designate successors but prevent them from having enough responsibility to learn how to do the job—what we might call the Prince Albert syndrome, remembering that Queen Victoria did not permit her son many opportunities to practice being king. This pattern is particularly likely to operate with a father-to-son transition.

When senior management or the founder confronts the criteria for a successor, cultural issues are forced into the open. It is now clear that much of the culture has become an attribute and property of the organization, even though it may have started out as the property of the founder. If the founder or family is still dominant in the organization, one may expect little culture change but a great deal of effort to clarify, integrate, maintain, and evolve the culture, primarily because it is identified with the founder.

When the founder or family finally relinquishes control, formal management succession provides an opportunity to change the direction of the culture if the successor is the right kind of hybrid, that is, if he represents what is needed for the organization to survive, yet is acceptable because he is one of us and therefore is also a conserver of parts of the old culture. In some companies, after several outsiders have failed as CEOs someone is found who was with the company earlier and therefore perceived by the family to understand the company—even though she brought in many new assumptions about how to run the business.

If the succession process is not managed effectively, founders and founding families lose power and are eventually replaced by formal means. If ownership becomes public, a board primarily made up of outsiders is created and a professional manager from outside the organization becomes the CEO. As family influence declines and the board goes on appointing CEOs, organizations enter what I think of as their midlife. As we shall see, the culture issues in midlife are quite different.

Practical Implications

- If you are in an organization that is still run by its founder, begin to build processes to examine and discuss succession.
- If you observe that the succession discussion is resisted or the founder exhibits symptoms of not wanting to face it, think in terms of providing insight in a low-key way by examining the succession process itself as a cultural artifact.
- Since you are dealing with powerful psychological forces regarding this issue, function as much as possible as a process consultant helping the CEO gain insight—not as a confrontational culture change agent.

The Bottom Line

Cultural change and the role of leadership in managing it occur through different mechanisms depending on the developmental stage of an organization. In the founding and early development stage, cultural assumptions define the group's identity and distinctive competence and hence are strongly held. If leaders detect maladaptive assumptions, the only way they can change culture is to bias the normal evolutionary processes, or produce therapeutic interventions that give group members new insight and thereby allow them to evolve their culture more manageably. The other major mechanism available to leaders in this stage is to locate and systematically promote hybrids in the organization who represent the main elements of the culture but who have learned some other assumptions in various subgroups that are considered adaptive.

The transition to midlife is fraught with cultural issues because succession problems force cultural assumptions out into the open. Group members are likely to confuse elements of the culture with elements of the founder's personality, and subgroups are likely to form for or against some of what the founder stands for. Cultural issues thus become salient during the transition of succession, but the change mechanisms are likely to be the same as the ones I have described, unless in the transition the company is sold or taken over by completely new management, in which case a new culture formation process begins.

The key issue for culture change leaders is that *they must become marginal in their own culture* sufficiently to recognize what may be its strengths worth preserving and its maladaptive assumptions requiring change. This demands the ability to learn new ways of thinking, as a prelude to unfreezing and changing their organization. This process is especially difficult for entrepreneurial founders because the early success of their organization is likely to make them believe that their own assumptions are ultimately the correct ones.

Chapter Six

Transformative Change

Unlearning and Relearning Culture

Before you can manage culture change in organizational midlife, you must first understand something about transformative change in general. In Chapter Five, I outlined *evolutionary* change mechanisms. But once cultural elements have stabilized, the change problem grows more complicated. It now involves having to *unlearn* beliefs, attitudes, values, and assumptions as well as learning new ones. People resist change because such unlearning is uncomfortable and anxiety-producing. They can be coerced into changing their overt behavior, but such behavior change is not stable unless the deeper levels undergo some kind of transformation. We have to look at what we know about change processes that are genuinely transformative.

A Simplifying Model of the Psychodynamics of Transformative Change

The model shown in Exhibit 6.1 involves three main stages and several substages that are described in some detail here. Without understanding the psychological and sociological dynamics that are involved, you cannot really grasp why culture change is so difficult in organizational midlife, or why it takes so many years. In this chapter, I explain the model; in Chapter Seven I provide case materials to illustrate the concepts.

Disconfirmation

Changing something implies not just learning something new but *unlearning* something that is already there and possibly in the way. What most learning theories and models overlook are the dynamics of unlearning, of overcoming resistance to change. They assume that if you can just get a clear enough vision of a positive future, this is motivation enough to get new learning started.

To respond to this belief, let's start by raising a controversial point. Is there a *natural instinct* to learn and improve? Or does there have to be some new motivating force before transformative learning begins to happen? Is natural curiosity enough of a motive to try new things and overcome old habits of thought? Or must there be some sense of dissatisfaction for motivation to arise? Does the dissatisfaction have to express itself as "survival anxiety" (I will not survive in some sense unless I change), or as "guilt" (I will not achieve my own ideals and aspirations unless I change)?

The organizational version of this question is, "Can a *successful* organization make major changes, or does there have to be some threat or sense of failure or crisis before people are motivated to make changes?" To use an analogy from offshore oil exploration,

Exhibit 6.1 A Model of Transformative Change

Stage One

Unfreezing: creating the motivation to change

- Disconfirmation
- Creation of survival anxiety or guilt
- Creation of psychological safety to overcome learning anxiety

Stage Two

Learning new concepts and new meanings for old concepts

- Imitation of and identification with role models
- Scanning for solutions and trial-and-error learning

Stage Three

Internalizing new concepts and meanings

- Incorporation into self-concept and identity
- Incorporation into ongoing relationships

must there be a burning platform before the need for real change is accepted? In sum, does the process of change or learning *always* have to start with some form of survival anxiety?

You undoubtedly have your own experience and bias, and no one has really been able to prove whether one or the other answer is correct. My own experience convinces me that some sense of threat, crisis, or dissatisfaction has to be present in a mature system in which things have to be unlearned before new things can be learned. Kurt Lewin, the social psychologist who did some of the most creative work in this area, thought of this as a process of "unfreezing." Human systems tend toward trying to maintain a stable equilibrium. If change is to occur, some new forces must upset the equilibrium; recognizing and managing these forces creates the motivation to change. *Any* change, then, begins with some *disconfirmation*.

Dissatisfaction and Threat as Sources of Disconfirmation

Members of the organization can experience these unfreezing forces directly, or they can be articulated by someone in the organization (usually in a high position) who functions as the motivator, the change leader. Disconfirming information can involve any or all of the following categories:

- An *economic* threat—unless you change, you will go out of business, lose market share, or suffer some other loss
- A *political* threat—unless you change, some more powerful group will win out over you or gain some advantage
- A *technological* threat—unless you change, you will be obsolete
- A *legal* threat—unless you change, you will go to jail or pay heavy fines
- A *moral* threat—unless you change, you will be seen as selfish, evil, socially irresponsible
- An *internal* discomfort—unless you change, you will not achieve some of your own goals and ideals

This last force, the internal one, is often thought of as the basis of "spontaneous" or natural learning, in that we seem to be able to motivate ourselves. We have a desire to do better, to achieve some ideal. But in my experience such spontaneously motivated learning is almost always triggered by some new information that signals failure to achieve our own goals and ideals. In other words, survival anxiety often shows up as a feeling of guilt that one is not achieving some values or ideals that one holds.

Scandal as a Source of Disconfirmation

For a corporation, one of the most powerful triggers to change is the occurrence of an accident (consider the Three Mile Island, *Challenger*, and Bhopal explosions) or a scandal (such as a price-fixing exposé or an executive suicide). What these events reveal is that some of the ideals and values the organization espouses turn out not to be operational in practice. This leads to reassessment of what the deeper cultural assumptions are that are actually operating. For example, a company that prided itself on a career system that gave managers real choice in overseas assignments had to face reality when a key overseas executive killed himself, and his suicide note revealed he had been pressured into the assignment despite personal and family objections to it. At the level of espoused values, the company had idealized its system. The scandal exposed the shared tacit assumption by which they really operated: that people were expected to go where senior executives wanted them to go. Recognizing the discrepancy then led to a whole program of revamping the career assignment system to bring espoused values and assumptions in line.

Mergers, Acquisitions, and Joint Ventures as Sources of Disconfirmation

The most obvious source of information that a change of culture is needed is when two or more cultures come together and try to work in concert. Unfortunately, in most cases the need for culture change arises only after the joint organization has been created, without consideration of whether the existing cultures were or were not compatible. The issue is then how the two cultures should relate to each other:

- Should they be allowed to *coexist independently*, as when a company acquires another but leaves it entirely alone?
- Should one culture *impose itself* on the other?
- Should the cultures be *blended* to attempt to maximize what are seen to be the strengths of each?

These pattern are found in the experiences of many companies. But there is some evidence that even in fifty-fifty mergers, blending is the pattern that is hardest to implement. Independent coexistence or cultural takeover are the more common patterns (Salk, 1992). More about this later.

Charismatic Leadership as a Source of Disconfirmation

A new leader who is charismatic can sometimes trigger survival anxiety or guilt by pointing out convincingly that "We are doing OK, but think how much better we could be doing if we learned how to do things in this new way. . . ." It takes charisma to get employees' attention, to avoid a complacent reaction that the bosses are only crying wolf. When a less-charismatic leader tries to convince the organization it is in trouble and must learn how to do some things differently in order to survive or grow, the message is often met with skepticism. Employees do not agree with the leaders' definition of *trouble*. They do not believe the organization is in economic, political, technological, or legal trouble, especially if those leaders give themselves generous bonuses while touting cost cutting. Employees often do not understand the economic situation well enough because they have never been educated in the economics of their business. Or they do not trust management, believing instead that if they work harder or smarter they will ultimately be taken advantage of anyway. What makes charismatic leaders so powerful is their ability to overcome this skepticism.

Education and Training as Sources of Disconfirmation

Many organizations have learned that the only way to convince employees and managers of the need to do things differently is by educational interventions. Especially in regard to the economics of the organization, employees do not believe what their leaders tell them unless they are educated to the economic realities of their business. A similar issue arises with respect to becoming responsible in the areas of environment, health, and safety. Employees do not accept the need for new, responsible behavior patterns until they have been educated to the dangers inherent in environmental events. Change programs therefore often have to begin with educational efforts, which may take time and energy.

Practical Implication

By definition, focusing on disconfirming events means you address the business problem before you even start to think about culture. You must have a clear definition of the business problem or issue that started the change process.

The disconfirming data are not the problem, however. They are only symptoms, which should trigger some diagnostic work. You have to think carefully about what the data are telling you and what the underlying problem or issue might be that needs to be addressed. Differentiate carefully between symptoms and possible underlying causes. Consider multiple causes; looking for one root cause is often a waste of time because of the degree to which causal forces may be interrelated.

It is in this analysis that you may first encounter the need for some culture assessment to determine how extensively cultural elements are involved in the problem situation. But stay focused on the business problem; avoid the temptation to blame the symptoms on the culture.

Survival Anxiety (or Guilt) Versus Learning Anxiety

If the disconfirming data get through your denial and defensiveness, you feel either survival anxiety or guilt. You recognize the need to change, the need to give up some old habits and ways of thinking, and the necessity of learning new habits and ways of thinking. But the minute you accept the need to change, you also begin to experience *learning anxiety*. The interaction of these two anxieties creates the complex dynamics of change.

The easiest way to illustrate this dynamic is in terms of learning a new stroke in tennis or golf. The process starts with disconfirmation: you are no longer winning against opponents you used to beat, or your aspirations for a better score or a better-looking game are not met. So you feel the need to improve your game. But as you contemplate the actual process of unlearning your old stroke or swing and developing a new one, you realize that you may not be able to do it, or you may be temporarily incompetent during the learning process. These feelings are learning anxiety. Similar feelings arise in the cultural arena when the new learning involves becoming computer competent; changing supervisory style; transforming competitive relationships into teamwork and collaboration; replacing a high-quality, high-cost strategy with one that leads to being the low-cost producer; moving from engineering domination and product orientation to a marketing-and-customer orientation; learning to work in nonhierarchical, diffuse networks; and so on.

Psychological Bases of Learning Anxiety

Learning anxiety is a combination of several specific fears, all of which may be active at any time as you contemplate having to unlearn something and learn something new.

Fear of Temporary Incompetence. During the transition process, you do not feel competent because you have given up the old way and have not yet mastered the new one. The best examples probably are evident in efforts to learn to use a computer.

Fear of Punishment for Incompetence. If it takes you a long time to learn the new way of thinking and doing things, you will fear being punished for your lack of productivity. In the computer arena, there are striking cases in which employees never learn the new system sufficiently to take advantage of its potential because they feel they have to remain productive—so they spend insufficient time on the new learning.

Fear of Loss of Personal Identity. If your current way of thinking is a strong source of identity for you, you may not wish to be the kind of person that the new culture requires you to be. For example, in the breakup of the Bell System many old-time employees left because they could not accept the identity of being a member of a hard-driving, cost-conscious organization that would take phones away from consumers who could not afford them.

Fear of Loss of Group Membership. The shared assumptions that make up a culture also identify who is in and who is out of the group. In developing new ways of thinking, you become a deviant in your group and may be rejected, or even ostracized. To avoid losing group membership, you resist learning the new ways of thinking and behaving. This fourth force is perhaps the most difficult to overcome because it requires the whole group to change how it thinks, as well as its norms of inclusion and exclusion.

Defensive Responses to Learning Anxiety

As long as your learning anxiety remains high, you are motivated to resist the validity of the disconfirming data or invent various excuses for why you cannot really engage in a transformative learning process right now. These responses come in definable stages.

Denial. You convince yourself that the disconfirming data are not valid, or are temporary, or don't really count, or reflect someone just crying "wolf," and so on.

Scapegoating, Passing the Buck, and Dodging. You convince yourself that the cause is in some other department, that the data do not apply to you, and that others need to change first before you do.

Maneuvering and Bargaining. You want special compensation for the effort to make the change; you want to be convinced that it is in your own interest and of long-range benefit to you.

Two Principles of Transformative Change

If you are the target of change confronted with the need to unlearn and relearn, you will resist in order to protect your position, your identity, and your group memberships even if it means experiencing survival anxiety or guilt. Your resistance is based on your learning anxiety. How, then, does the change manager create transformative change? Two principles come into play:

Principle One: Survival anxiety or guilt must be greater than learning anxiety

Principle Two: Learning anxiety must be reduced rather than increasing survival anxiety

From the change manager's point of view, it might seem obvious that the way to motivate you would be simply to increase the survival anxiety or make you feel even more guilty about failing to achieve your ideals. The problem with this approach is that with greater threat or guilt you may simply increase your defensiveness to avoid the threat or pain of the learning process. That logic leads to the key insight about transformative change embodied in principle two: learning anxiety must be reduced by increasing the learner's sense of *psychological safety*.

How Do You Create Psychological Safety?

Creating psychological safety for organizational members who are undergoing transformational learning involves a number of steps, and they must be taken almost simultaneously. I list them here chronologically, but the change manager must be prepared to implement all of them.

1. A *compelling positive vision*. If you are the target of change, you must believe that you and the organization will be better off if you learn the new way of thinking and working. The vision must be articulated (and widely held) by senior management.

2. *Formal training*. If you are to learn new ways of thinking, new attitudes, and new skills, you must have access to whatever formal training is required. For example, if the new way of working necessitates teamwork, formal training on team building and maintenance must be provided.

3. *Involvement of the learner*. If the formal training is to take hold, you must have a sense that you can manage your own informal method of learning. Everyone learns slightly differently, so it is essential to involve learners in designing their own optimal learning process.

4. *Informal training of relevant "family" groups and teams*. Because cultural assumptions are embedded in groups, informal training and practice must be provided to whole groups so that new norms and new assumptions can be built jointly. You should not feel deviant in deciding to engage in the new learning.

5. *Practice fields, coaches, and feedback*. You cannot learn something fundamentally new if you don't have the time, the resources, coaching, and valid feedback on how you are doing. Practice fields are particularly important so that you can make mistakes and learn from them without disrupting the organization.

6. *Positive role models*. The new way of thinking and behaving may be so different that you must see what it looks like before you can imagine yourself doing it. You must be able to see the new behavior and attitudes in others with whom you can identify.

7. *Support groups*. Groups should be formed in which problems connected with learning are aired and discussed. You must be able to talk about your frustrations and difficulties in learning with others who are experiencing similar difficulties so that you can support each other and jointly learn new ways of dealing with the difficulties.

8. *Consistent systems and structures*. It is essential to have reward and discipline systems and organizational structures consistent with the new way of thinking and working. For example, if you are learning how to be a team player, the reward system must be group-oriented, the discipline system must punish individually

aggressive and selfish behavior, and the organizational structures must make it possible to work as a team.

Most transformational change programs fail because they do not create these eight conditions. If you consider the difficulty of achieving all eight, and the energy and resources that have to be expended to accomplish them, it is small wonder that changes are often short-lived or never get going at all. On the other hand, as some of the cases in the next chapter show, when an organization sets out to truly transform itself, real and significant cultural changes can be achieved.

Cognitive Redefinition

The best way to characterize the process of what actually happens in the learner is to call it *cognitive redefinition*. If you have been trained to think in a certain way and are a member of a group that thinks the same way, how can you imagine changing to a new way of thinking? If you are an engineer at Beta Oil, you are a member of a division that used to work as experts with technical resources, clear career lines, and a single boss. In the new structure, you are now asked to think of yourself as a member of a consulting organization that sells its services to customers who can purchase them elsewhere if they do not like your deal. To make such a transformation, first you must develop several *new* concepts: "freelance consultant," "selling services for a fee," "competing with outsiders who can underbid you." In addition, you have to learn a new meaning for the concept of being an engineer, and what it now means to be an employee of Beta Oil. You face a new reward system, and being paid and promoted on your ability to bring in work. You must now see yourself as a salesman more than an engineer. Finally, you must define your career in quite different terms and learn to work for lots of bosses.

Along with new concepts come new standards of evaluation. Whereas in the former structure you were evaluated largely on the quality of your work, you now have to estimate more accurately just how many days a given job will take, what quality level can be achieved in that time, and what it costs if you try for the higher-quality standard you are used to.

The computer designers at DEC who tried to develop products competitive with the IBM PC never changed their standards of evaluation for what a customer expected. They overdesigned the products, made them too expensive, and included far too many bells and whistles. The designers were embedded in their old way of thinking, and the organization did not have a change program powerful enough to help them cognitively redefine what the new marketplace needed.

When senior management announces a strategy of shifting from a production or engineering focus to a customer-centered marketing focus, they are asking many of their employees to make a major cognitive shift that they may not be able to make. When senior management announces they are going from a formal hierarchy to a matrix or networked project structure, they are asking their employees to grasp entirely alien concepts of how to work and how to think about authority. When senior management announces that employees should become more involved and empowered, they are asking both employees and supervisors to shift their whole cognitive frame of reference for what it means to be an employee or a supervisor.

Such cognitive shifts are possible if the organization manages to create enough psychological safety—especially if it involves the people who are the targets of change in the learning process. Then the learning takes place through either trial and error (based on the learner's scanning of the work environment to locate possible options for new behaviors) or a more formal training process (which usually involves imitating role models and psychologically identifying with them).

Imitation and Identification Versus Scanning and Trial and Error

There are, then, basically two mechanisms by which you learn new concepts, new meanings for old concepts, and new standards of evaluation. You learn through imitating a role model and psychologically identifying with that person. Or you keep inventing your own solutions until something works for you.

If you are the change manager, you have a choice as to which mechanism to encourage. As part of a training program, you can provide role models through case materials, films, role plays, or simulations. You can bring in learners who have acquired the new concepts and encourage others to find out how they did it. This mechanism works best if it is clear what the new way of working is to be and if the concepts to be taught are themselves clear. However, we sometimes learn things through imitation only to find that they do not really fit into our personality or our ongoing relationships. Once we are on our own and the role models are no longer available, we revert to our old behavior.

Alternatively, if you want the learners to learn things that really fit into their personality, then you must withhold role models and encourage learners to scan their environment and develop their own solutions. For example, Beta Oil could have developed a training program for how to be a consultant, built around engineers who had made the shift successfully. However, senior management felt that the shift was so personal that they decided merely to create the structure and the incentives, but let each engineer figure out for himself or herself how to manage the new kinds of relationships. In some cases, this meant people left the organization. But those engineers who learned from their own experience how to be consultants genuinely evolved to a new kind of career, one that they integrated into their total life.

The general principle here is that *the change manager must be clear* about the ultimate goals, the new way of working that is to be achieved. But this does not necessarily imply that everyone gets to the goal in the same way. Involving the learner does not imply that the learner has a choice about the ultimate *goals*, but it does imply personal choice of the *means* to get there.

Refreezing

The final step in any transformative change process is to internalize the new concepts leading to new behavior. If the behavior fits the rest of the personality and is congruent with the expectations of important others in the learner's work and social environment, it becomes a stable part of the person, and eventually of the group. But note that if you learn some new concepts that lead to new behavior that does *not* fit into your work or social group, you will either revert to your old concepts and behavior if you value the group, or leave the group if you now value the new concepts and behavior more.

Practical Implications

If you are the change manager, you must think carefully about which outcomes you want. First, you must decide whether entire groups or units must adopt the new way. In most culture change programs, it is almost always the case that you want the entire work unit to adopt a new way of thinking and behaving; so the training should initially be geared to groups, not individuals.

As you examine the entire organization whose culture is to be changed, think in terms of the various workgroups, hierarchical levels, departments, geographical units, and so on. If only key individuals change, chances are that when they go back to their workgroups they will revert to the norms of those groups.

Second, you must decide whether or not the new way of thinking and behaving can be more or less standardized. If there is clear consensus on the new way, then you should provide role models and behavioral examples of the new way of thinking and behaving. This process speeds up the learning but also leads to adopting new behaviors that may not fit the learners, that fail to be internalized, and that are eventually abandoned. On the other hand, you can state clear goals but invite learners to develop their own solutions. This trial and error is a slower process, but it guarantees that whatever is learned is internalized. In this instance, you should withhold role models or clear examples.

Temporary Parallel Learning Systems

Evolutionary learning and change goes on all the time. Organizations are dynamic systems interacting with perpetually changing environments. Transformational change becomes an issue when the level of disconfirmation forces senior management to examine fundamental assumptions about how it is operating. Often such an examination reveals that the problems can be fixed without having to change elements of the culture. If, however, senior management recognizes that elements of the culture have become dysfunctional, then it must launch a transformational change program and create a management process that makes such deep change feasible.

The actual change activities will vary according to the situation, but almost all such programs involve creating a temporary parallel learning system in which some new assumptions are learned and tested (Bushe and Shani, 1991; Zand, 1974). It is too painful to give up a shared assumption in favor of an unknown substitute. If some part of the organization can learn an alternative way of thinking, and if the alternative can be shown to work, then there is less anxiety as the alternative is gradually introduced into the main part of the organization. The trial and error in the temporary parallel system creates some of the necessary psychological safety by providing role models for new ways of thinking and behaving.

The essence of the concept of a temporary parallel system is that some part of the organization must become marginal and expose itself to new ways of thinking so that it can be objective about the strengths and weaknesses of the existing cultural elements, and how these will aid or hinder the changes to be made.

Fully engaged insiders simply cannot see the culture in which they are embedded clearly enough to assess and evaluate its elements. On the other hand, having an entirely outside assessment of the culture is equally unlikely to be productive because the outsider does not know enough of the cultural nuances to be able to make an assessment. The solution is for the parallel system to include key insiders who then work with consultants to decipher the culture and plan the change program.

The parallel system is usually a task force, including senior leadership and key members of groups that are going to feel the impact of the transformational change. Assignment to the task force is usually at least a half-time job, and often full-time. The task force requires time, a budget, and whatever other resources ensure that a thorough job of assessment and planning is done. If the change program is extensive, the original task force may become a steering committee that "owns" the whole program. But the implementation may then involve a whole series of other task forces that function as parallel systems vis-à-vis the various groups involved in the change process. It is the steering committee and its various offshoots that I have been labeling *change teams*. How this works in practice is illustrated in the cases in Chapter Seven.

All of these transformational programs have in common that they are planned and consciously managed by the leaders of the organization, such that periods of disequilibrium are anticipated as a normal part of organizational evolution rather than as painful disruptions. It is also assumed that the organization cannot learn anything new if the leaders themselves do not. Leaders need to be made marginal, to have some new insights, and to participate in the parallel system to explore the new learning in a wider context.

If basic assumptions are really to be changed without destroying and rebuilding the organization, transformations require anywhere from five to fifteen years or more. It takes time to construct the parallel system, learn new assumptions, and then design processes that allow the assumptions to be introduced into the original organization. Recall the Procter & Gamble example from Chapter One; it took fifteen years for all of the plants to convert to the new manufacturing system.

The Work of the Change Team

Once a change team is designated, how does it structure the work? The best model of the stages and elements of the change process is the map developed by Beckhard and Harris (1987), as shown in Figure 6.1.

What Is the Ideal Future State?

The first element in the change map is a reminder to confirm that change is needed and feasible. Change leaders must not only examine the level of disconfirmation and their own motives, but also make a broad judgment about what kind of change is feasible. Carefully thinking through the problem that underlies the disconfirming symptoms is a crucial step in this first stage of the change process.

If a change is needed and is deemed possible, the next step is to define the ideal future state. The definition must be clear and concrete. It should answer this question:

> If you are to solve the business problem or achieve the ideals that are not being met, what are the new ways of thinking and working that will get you there?

Figure 6.1 A Map of the Change Management Process

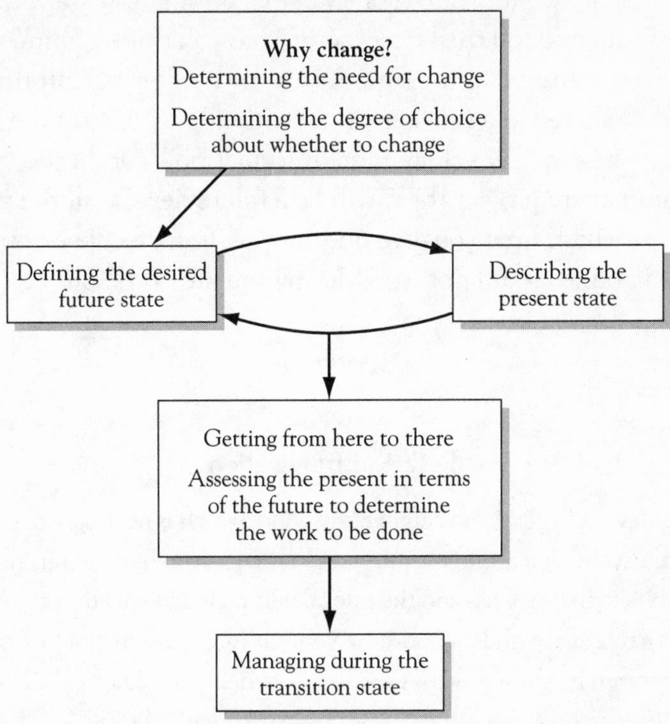

Adapted from Beckhard and Harris, 1987.

Unless you can specify just what behavioral changes are ultimately needed, you cannot test the relevance of culture to the change process. All too often, leaving the ideal state vague means discovering too late that there is no way to get there from the present culture. This implies that the new way of thinking and working has to be specified very concretely. It is not enough to say that in the future "we need more teamwork," or "from now on we will be more open with each other." You must say that in the new way of working, every team is measured and rewarded as a team. You have to specify which tasks require a high level of interdependence and, therefore, what kind of teamwork. In the area of openness, specify what kinds of information must be openly transmitted, when, and by what means. For example, do you now want to let it all hang out and tell the boss exactly what you think of him or her? Or do you intend by openness that task-relevant information should be shared in a timely manner with all members of the team? Do you just say, "Let's share more information"? Or do you specify that after every project there will be a full review by all the participants at which time you give one another frank feedback on what worked and what did not work during the life of the project?

Practical Implication

To develop a clear and compelling vision, which is necessary to create psychological safety, you have to be clear about the business problem to be solved and the role of culture. Paradoxically, the best way to clearly understand how your culture is implicated in the change is not to start with the idea of changing the culture. Instead, concentrate on what the new way of working is to be.

Based on the change leader's vision and your own understanding of where the organization is trying to go, bring together a change team, or start a series of focus group meetings to define what kind of behavior you expect in some future ideal state you are striving for. Be as concrete as you can in specifying the new behavior, and think of many examples to share with employees as part of their education.

The change map forces you to think clearly about why you are making the change in the first place, how feasible it is, and what ideal state you are trying to achieve. In defining the ideal state, it is often desirable to use "appreciative inquiry," to focus on what is working and how to enhance it rather than on problems (Barrett and Cooperrider, 1990).

Only after you have figured out the ideal future state in terms of the new way of thinking and working are you ready to do the culture assessment.

Assessing the Present State

Once the ideal state is well understood, the change team must diagnose and assess the present state of the system to determine what the gap is between the ideal future and the present. In assessing the present state, it is especially important to create a parallel system to ensure objectivity. A change team of all insiders is likely to misperceive the state of the culture, or not perceive it at all because team members are so embedded in it. The cultural assessment processes described earlier in this book are appropriate and necessary at this point.

Practical Implications

You are ready to do the culture assessment once you are clear on the business problem and the new way of working that derives from your vision of the ideal state. First, focus the assessment on how the present culture can help you achieve the new way of working. Second, identify cultural elements that may hinder achievement of your goals, and design a specific program of culture change to deal with those elements. Remind yourself that you are not changing the entire culture, only elements that hinder your change program.

Making the Change Target Concrete

As the change team works on the ideal state and the present state, it probably has to periodically redefine the change problem in terms of the gap or gaps identified. In other words, though the process is a set of steps undertaken in sequence, there are many feedback loops that force going back to earlier steps to guarantee clear thinking. The best way to state the gap is to concretely specify how thinking and working is done in the present and contrast that with a clear statement of what the new way of thinking and working is to be. For example, it is not enough to say "we need more collaboration and teamwork in the sales division." State the gap in terms like this: "In the present system, we have sales divisions competing with each other to meet their own targets." Then, for the future ideal state: "We want to have sales divisions collaborate across geographies on the large accounts that are themselves spread across those geographies." To take a second instance, the gap is that "we currently reward each salesman by meeting individual targets"; the future ideal state is that "we should develop a compensation system that makes the sales groups want to work together on the large, geographically dispersed accounts."

As various gaps are identified in concrete form, it becomes apparent where cultural assumptions aid or hinder the change agenda. For example, having sales teams work together on big accounts may sound simple until it is discovered that the organization's individualistic culture prevents changing the incentive system to a group-based compensation program. The change program then has to shift to examining how to change some of the individualistic assumptions; this might entail an entirely new change program not previously thought about at all.

Developing a Transition Plan and Change Management Process

As gaps are identified concretely, the change team sees what kind of actual change process is needed. For this stage, there are no pat solutions or overarching models. Rather, the change team has to use its own design and intervention skills, or else bring in process consultants, to design the next steps. They might be educational intervention of various sorts, creation of new task forces, large system interventions, team building or other workshop processes, and coaching of key executives.

At this point, the change team often becomes more of a steering committee and launches other teams and management processes to promote forward progress. The change team and its leaders must continue to own the whole transformation and remain accountable, but it usually delegates work to various other groups and monitors that carry out their work periodically.

Practical Implications

Try not to short-circuit the above steps. The temptation to launch into action is tremendous, but where culture is involved it is better to go slow initially and make sure you have figured out what the new way of thinking and working is, and how the culture can aid or hinder you before you launch major new initiatives. It is especially important to figure out how the culture can aid you—how you can build on the present culture to accomplish the needed changes.

Revisit the concept of psychological safety: how to make the people who are the targets of change sufficiently motivated to want to change but not so anxious about learning new things as to resist change. Here again, figure out how the present culture can help the learning process and make people feel secure.

Change Leaders and Change Agents

Change leaders can be thought of as persons who create enough disconfirmation in the organization to arouse motivation to change. Change leaders should therefore have three characteristics if they are to arouse motivation to change and learn:

1. *Credibility.* Whatever they say must be believed (not discounted).
2. *Clarity of vision.* Whatever they say must be clear and make sense.
3. *Ability to articulate the vision.* They must be able to state verbally and in writing what it is they perceive and what

the implications are for the future of the organization (Bennis and Nanus, 1985, Kouzes and Posner, 1995).

Once motivation is present, *change agents* (what I called earlier the change team) can proceed with developing various processes to make it happen. Change agents may or may not be the same persons as the change leaders. They do *not* need to be in positions of formal leadership; in fact, they often work more effectively as catalysts and facilitators rather than overtly as leaders (if there is already some source of motivation present). Their most important role is to implement the various steps described in the Beckhard/Harris map (Figure 6.1).

Change leaders can articulate new directions, new values, and new visions, but it is usually the change team, functioning as a temporary parallel system, that defines exactly what is required of the organization in terms of new thinking and behavior. The change team, then, must be able to function as process consultants, simultaneously diagnosing and intervening as they work through the stages of change (Schein, 1987, 1999).

The Bottom Line

This chapter focuses on the dynamics of transformative change. First, we reviewed the psychological and social dynamics involved in any change process that requires unlearning as well as new learning. The key is to understand that resistance to change is to be expected as a normal phenomenon, and that new learning only takes place if the learner is made to feel psychologically secure. In terms of a principle for transformative change, survival anxiety has to be greater than learning anxiety; but a second principle is that the preferred way to achieve this state is to reduce learning anxiety. In examining all the conditions needed to create psychological safety, it becomes clear why transformative change is difficult and time consuming.

Second, we reviewed how a change team must become a temporary parallel system that manages the entire change process in terms of the stages identified by Beckhard and Harris. I emphasize that the change goal—the new way of thinking and behaving—must be specified quite concretely in order to determine how the present culture will aid or hinder the change process. The more one can use the culture as an aid, the easier it is to achieve the change. If cultural elements are found to be hindrances, then new change processes have to be designed to deal with them. But one should not automatically assume that every change is a culture change. How this all works is illustrated in the cases in Chapter Seven.

Chapter Seven

Corporate Culture Dynamics in the Mature Company

- From Ownership to General Management Structures
- Culture Change Mechanisms in Organizational Midlife
- Planned and Managed Culture Change
- Organizational Midlife Crisis and Potential Decline
- Drastic Culture Change
- The Bottom Line

Organizational midlife or maturity creates a series of cultural issues that differ dramatically from the issues of growth and early evolution. As I pointed out in the last chapter, we are now dealing with unlearning and replacing assumptions and values, and we are dealing with stable, highly differentiated cultures that are likely to be both functional in some parts and dysfunctional in other parts. The mechanisms of change differ as well because the management structures in mature organizations are not those of founder-led and founder-owned organizations.

From Ownership to General Management Structures

The most salient characteristic of organizational midlife is that the management processes are created by *promoted general managers*, not entrepreneurs, founders, or founding families.

When the founding family is no longer in an ownership or dominant position, or after at least two generations of general management, or when the organization has grown in size to the point where the sheer number of nonfamily managers overweighs the family members, we are talking about midlife and maturity.

In building their businesses, founders and founding families often hold values other than purely economic ones. They impose these values on the organization and embed them in the culture. On the other hand, general managers who have worked their way up in the organization usually learn that humanistic, environmental, spiritual, and other noneconomic values have to be subordinated to the pragmatic problems of running the business and keeping it financially viable. Promoted managers do not have the luxury that founder-owners enjoy of taking financial risks to preserve certain of their values and beliefs. Promoted general managers are usually more vulnerable to powerful outside boards; they have shorter tenures and learn how to survive in organizations. As CEOs, they typically come into their jobs when the organization is already highly differentiated in terms of subcultures.

As such managers rise and take on greater responsibilities, they also discover the painful reality that managing people is gradually displaced by managing systems and processes. As one CEO of a consumer goods industry put it:

> I started out as a store manager, where I knew all of my people very well. When I was promoted to a district with ten stores, I visited all of the stores on a regular basis and still knew the several hundred people who worked in them. But then, when I was promoted to regional and eventually division manager, I discovered I could no longer know enough of the people in the stores to feel personally attached. I had to invent systems, procedures, and rules and implement them through my immediate subordinates. But at this stage it felt like a completely different kind of job and became much more impersonal. This was the most important transition in my managerial career.

From a cultural perspective, the midlife organization faces a very different situation. It is established and must maintain itself through some kind of continued growth-and-renewal process. It must decide whether to pursue such growth through further geographical expansion, development of new products, opening up of new markets, vertical integration to improve its cost and resource positions, mergers and acquisitions, divisionalization, or spin-offs. The past history of the organization's growth and development is not necessarily a good guide to what will succeed in the future because the environment is likely to change; more important, internal changes are likely to alter the organization's unique strengths and weaknesses.

Whereas culture was a necessary glue in the period of growth, the most important elements of the culture are now embedded in the structure and major processes of the organization. Hence, consciousness of the culture and deliberate attempts to build, integrate, or conserve the culture are less important. *The culture that the organization acquired during its early years is now taken for granted*. The only elements that are likely to be conscious are the credos, dominant espoused values, company slogans, written charters, and other public pronouncements of what the company wants to be and claims to stand for—its philosophy and ideology.

Whereas leadership created culture in the early stages, *culture now creates leaders*, in the sense that only those managers who fit the mold are promoted to top positions. In fact, one of the most dangerous aspects of culture at this stage is that it is an unconscious determinant of most of what goes on in the organization, including even the mission and strategy of the organization.

At this stage, it is more difficult to decipher the culture and make people aware of it because it is so embedded in routines. Raising awareness of the culture may even be counterproductive unless there is some crisis or specific problem to be solved. Managers view culture discussions as boring and irrelevant, especially if the company is large and well established. On the other hand, if the organization undertakes geographical expansions, mergers and acquisitions, joint ventures, and/or introduces new technologies, it must do a careful self-assessment to determine whether the existing culture is compatible with the new ways of thinking and behaving that are to be introduced.

Also at this stage, there may be strong forces toward cultural diffusion and loss of integration. Powerful subcultures have developed, and a highly integrated culture is difficult to maintain in a large, differentiated, geographically dispersed organization. Furthermore, as the organization ages, it becomes less clear whether all the subcultural units of an organization should be uniform and integrated. Several conglomerates I have worked with spent a good deal of time wrestling with the question of whether to attempt to preserve, or in some cases build, a common culture. Are the costs associated with such an effort worth it? Is there even a danger of imposing assumptions on a subunit that might not fit the situation at all? On the other hand, if subunits are all allowed to develop their own cultures, what is the competitive advantage of being a single organization? Resolving such questions often requires careful assessment of the actual culture to see what elements, if any, should be generalized, given the varying tasks of the organizational units.

From a cultural perspective, then, the essence of the leader's job is not how to create an organizational culture but how to manage the diversity of subcultural forces that are already operating, that is, how to integrate and evolve a highly differentiated organization, and how to enhance elements of the culture that are congruent with new environmental realities while changing dysfunctional elements of the culture. If cultural elements have to be changed, then we are dealing with transformative change (as described in the last chapter); this requires mechanisms that go beyond the evolutionary ones characteristic of the young and growing organization.

Practical Implication

Spend a little time by yourself, or with some colleagues, reviewing the history of your company.

- Think back to the founders. Ask what deep values and assumptions they held that became part of the culture of the organization. If necessary, locate some old-timers who remember what the founding culture was like.

- Identify powerful leaders who came after the founders. Ask yourself whether or not they changed elements of the culture during their leadership period. If yes, in what way? What new ways of thinking and behaving did they introduce?
- Now shift your focus to the environment. Ask yourself how the economic, technological, political, and social environments in which your company operates have changed. To what extent are some of the deepest assumptions of your founders and early leaders no longer functional in the present environment?

This exercise gets you started in thinking about a more formal culture assessment, which you should do with a larger group according to the method described in Chapter Four.

Culture Change Mechanisms in Organizational Midlife

The culture change mechanisms described in Chapter Five (general and specific evolution, guided evolution through insight, managed evolution through promotion of hybrids, and empowering managers from selected subcultures) all continue to operate in midlife. But because culture is now more differentiated and embedded, if elements of the culture are potentially dysfunctional then the change mechanisms have to be more transformative than evolutionary. They involve unlearning old ways of thinking, a process that is fundamentally more threatening and that almost invariably creates resistance to change. Evolving the culture through systematic selection of managers from certain subcultures is often too slow a process to make the necessary transformations. The major change mechanism then becomes *planned and managed culture change*, through a systematic process involving change leaders and change teams operating as parallel structures.

Planned and Managed Culture Change

As the cases below illustrate, much of the work of the change manager and change team now concerns the psychological and sociological dynamics described in Chapter Six.

Cultural changes through planned change processes are more feasible in this stage because culture is no longer linked psychologically and emotionally to founders and family members. Whereas many managerial practices were sacred in the youthful period, it is now easier to assess those practices and the assumptions lying behind them objectively to determine their strengths and weaknesses. In other words, if you now believe that certain assumptions are dysfunctional, you are no longer criticizing a "father figure." Rather than being the glue and source of identity, culture becomes part of the tradition of success—the assumptions that brought the organization to where it is today. This is still a strong conservative force because many employees and managers take it for granted that what worked to make the organization successful must still be right. Just announcing a new way of doing things, or new values, does not shake these convictions.

It is for this reason that you will still want to link whatever changes need to be made to *existing* cultural assumptions, rather than starting all over with the announcement of a new culture. Even if it appears that the necessary changes challenge deeply held assumptions, one of the most important parts of the assessment process described in the last chapter is to try to link future business practices to current cultural themes. It is far easier to link necessary changes to existing cultural themes than to try to change the culture. Effective organizations are able to evolve their practices in this manner around a small number of high-level core values and assumptions that do not change (Kotter and Heskett, 1992; Collins and Porras, 1994).

The trigger for this kind of change process is usually exposure of the organization to strongly disconfirming information leading to a decision by executive management that some major changes have to be made if the organization is to survive and continue to be successful. Change leaders emerge or are appointed, and change teams are formed. At various stages in the transformative process, the need for culture assessment arises; at those times the change team must decide how the culture can aid the change process as well as how to change cultural elements that may be dysfunctional. Further interventions are then planned in terms of the specific elements of the culture identified.

Note, however: the things that are perceived as disconfirming, the information that produces survival anxiety in executive management, and the remedial processes that they launch are themselves culturally determined. Therefore, every mature organization's change program reflects its own culture and is likely to differ from what another organization with its own culture might do. Consequently I cannot give you a blueprint for this kind of change, but only some cases from which we can infer a few broad generalizations. The underlying mechanics of change follow the model presented in the last chapter, but how they are implemented or experienced differs from company to company.

Case Example: Moderate Culture Change at "Alpha Power"

As you read the "Alpha Power" case, you should note several things. The major disconfirming force came from outside, which made internal change not only necessary but also more feasible. Some of the requisite culture changes are supported by structural changes, but as deeper layers of the culture are exposed it becomes unclear to what extent the company is willing to change the culture and its structural manifestations. You should also note how difficult it is to identify some of the deeper assumptions, how many of them reflect the deep division between management and the employees, and how hard it is to create sufficient psychological safety to make some of the changes possible.

> Alpha Power's change program started some years back when a power plant suffered an explosion and sprayed asbestos into the surrounding neighborhood. The local environmental agency brought

criminal charges against the company because it felt that the company had lied in denying that there had been any asbestos danger. The case was settled out of court with a consent order that required the company to:

1. Pay heavy fines
2. Institute a set of diagnostic and remedial environmental procedures, including periodic assessment of progress by outside consulting firms
3. Accept the presence of a court-appointed monitor, who would report to the judge and write quarterly appraisals of the progress of the company in meeting all of the environmental goals that had been set
4. Remain on probation for a period of three years, during which it would demonstrate becoming more environmentally responsible

One of the most stringent goals was to become more open and honest with the government in admitting environmental events and putting into place remedial measures.

The major unfreezing forces were the loss of autonomy that resulted from being on probation and the presence of the court-appointed monitor, whose quarterly reports reminded everyone in the company of what it was not doing to achieve its own vision.

At the same time, senior management came to an important realization. To be competitive in the future deregulated market, the kind of employee behavior that leads to responsible behavior with respect to environment, health, and safety issues (EH&S) would also be desirable to make the company generally more competitive.

Senior management, especially the well-respected and powerful CEO, clearly articulated a vision for employees to become more team-oriented, more open in their communications, more personally responsible, better at planning and risk assessment, and more capable of assessing and remedying EH&S issues. A senior vice president for environmental affairs was hired and charged with building an organization that would provide training, consulting, expertise in diagnosis and remediation, and—most important—some oversight to ensure that EH&S affairs were properly handled at every level. A high-level environmental committee (EHSC) was formed, with monthly meetings to assess progress in reducing environmental events, such as oil spills; set policy; and generally oversee the entire program.

In addition, an environmental quality review board (EQRB) was formed, consisting of two highly respected environmental lawyers whose job was to help the company with its problems of compliance. The board would also ensure that the program as it evolved would satisfy the U.S. attorney's office sufficiently to warrant recommendation that the probation be lifted at the end of the three-year period. I was added to the board as a "culture expert" when it became apparent from the monitor's quarterly reports that he viewed "the culture" of the company as being the major constraint to effective change in the EH&S area. We three members of this board were on the EHSC, which became in effect the parallel structure to examine how culture would aid or hinder the change effort. The fact that the committee had outsiders as well as high-ranking insiders made it de facto the steering committee for the entire transformation, and made it more "marginal."

My Role as the Culture Consultant

My mandate was to help Alpha figure out which elements of the culture were in the way of making the needed changes and to educate management on culture dynamics in general. I approached this as a process consultant, mindful that all of my interviews were themselves interventions into the system. At the same time, all of the exploratory interventions served as diagnostic indicators of what the culture was like. The examples provided by the monitor in his reports suggested that some of the very things that once made

Alpha successful might now be dysfunctional with respect to the CEO's newly articulated vision. For example, open reporting to the government might be completely alien in a culture built on tight group loyalties and keeping dirty laundry hidden from outsiders.

I spent several full days over a period of months interviewing groups of employees in the EH&S area, union employees who actually did the work in the streets, first-line supervisors, middle managers, and—most vitally—the entire senior management group. I needed to test whether the vision was shared by senior management and how well it was understood down the line. It was clear from these individual and group interviews that the basic vision and the need to become environmentally responsible were well understood and accepted, but there was little understanding of what the court monitor meant in stating that the company's culture stood in the way of actually achieving openness, teamwork, and EH&S responsibility.

It then became my job to:

1. Educate the company about the concept of culture and what is involved in culture change
2. Help the company define more clearly the new way of working if the above newly articulated values were to be achieved
3. Help the company define which elements in its culture would aid the change effort and which would hinder it
4. If elements of the culture were discovered to be a hindrance, help in developing a culture change program to deal with those elements

Educational Interventions

It was decided that after several months I should make a presentation to the EHSC, which would begin to educate them on the concept of culture. With the help of slides, I explained the basic steps that would be needed if the culture were to be changed. The talk was supplement by a set of notes, which presented the basic model of change that had to be learned. I present parts of these notes in

Exhibit 7.1 because they served as the blueprint for the entire change process under way at Alpha; they also illustrate how the change theory presented in the last chapter can be communicated to employees and managers. The essence of a good educational intervention is to get difficult concepts across concretely so that the audience can apply the theory to themselves immediately.

The presentation was discussed at length, and senior management began to appreciate how complex this change would be. Most important, I needed to test whether or not the group was still committed to culture change, given better understanding of what would be involved. They asserted that they were committed and followed up the assertion by scheduling a similar talk for the next layer of management below them. In the meantime, I continued to meet with groups that would help define what the cultural dilemma was at the employee level. In other words, if a new way of working was to be defined, what in the old way of working would get in the way? These elements of the culture gradually surfaced during the group interviews I held with employees.

Relevant Elements of the Present Culture

The elements of the old, or present, culture to be confronted are best characterized in terms of these historically evolved and widely shared norms and assumptions:

- Getting the power back on and maintaining reliable service is always the number one priority.
- The heroic way to be is to get the power on no matter what risks have to be taken or what formal procedures have to be ignored in the process.
- The heroic way to be is to respond to crises as they occur; careful planning and using noncrisis times to plan are not valued.
- You do what your boss tells you to do; supervisors organize the job and give the orders on how to do it.

(*text continues on page 155*)

Exhibit 7.1 Excerpts of Notes Presented to "Alpha Power" Change Committee

What Does It Take to Change Elements of Culture?

I. Motivation to change

Motivation is produced by *disconfirming information* that creates survival anxiety and guilt. What produces such feelings?

- *Actual external events*, such as explosions, injuries, or spills, that are expensive to clean up make members of the organization realize that something needs to change. *Survival anxiety* can be thought of as the anxiety that is produced by the prospect of not changing anything and hence becoming less adaptive or competitive.
- *Formal external disconfirmation* in the form of a court order, a court-appointed monitor's reports of violations, further accidents or spills, etc. This causes survival anxiety.
- *Internal recognition* that things are not as good as they could be, that corners are being cut, procedures are not being followed, ineffective performance is tolerated and ineffective employees are carried, standards of conduct are not enforced, and others who violate them are not disciplined. This causes guilt that ideals are not being met.

II. Why is disconfirmation not enough to start a change? (Learning anxiety and resistance to change)

Survival anxiety and guilt motivate one to learn something new, but at the same time, if the new behavior, attitude, value, etc. requires me to unlearn something I already know how to do, I immediately experience *learning anxiety*.

Learning anxiety is the combination of several specific fears:

- Fear that I will become temporarily incompetent while I learn something new (lack of understanding or skill in diagnosing and fixing environmental "stuff")

Exhibit 7.1 Excerpts of Notes Presented to "Alpha Power" Change Committee (*continued*)

- Fear that I will lose my sense of identity if I adopt new attitudes, values, and behavior (loss of capacity to be the macho person who gets and keeps the power on)
- Fear that I will lose my group identity if I deviate from previously accepted group norms (harassment, ostracism, and other group punishments for ratting, being too rule-bound, not minding my "own business," embarrassing coworkers or bosses or my organizational unit)
- Fear that I will be punished by the organization for taking too long, or going outside my specific prescribed duties; I might be unproductive while I am learning, which would make my boss mad

III. Defensive responses to learning anxiety

As long as learning anxiety remains high, I resist change and invent various reasons or excuses:

- *Defensive denial*: "They don't really mean it"; "It will all go away and we will be back to normal"; "They are just crying wolf"; "That wasn't really oil in the spill"; "Senior management just has to say all that stuff because of the court"; "The court will not really keep us on probation any more"; and so on.
- *Scapegoating, passing the buck, and dodging*: "It doesn't apply to me"; "We are in this trouble only because 'they' in that other department are the cause"; "The minor things we do hardly count compared to what they do"; and so on.
- *Bargaining and maneuvering*: "OK, I'll learn how to do the environmental thing, but you'll have to pay me more or you'll have to give me extra time to do my 'normal' job"; "If I follow the new rules and learn the new stuff, what's in it for me besides more work?" and so on.

Exhibit 7.1 Excerpts of Notes Presented to "Alpha Power" Change Committee (*continued*)

IV. Overcoming resistance to change by creating psychological safety

For new learning to occur, survival anxiety has to be greater than learning anxiety. But increasing survival anxiety by threatening people just increases their defensive resistance or leads only to surface compliance. To internalize learning, one needs to reduce learning anxiety by means of the following steps, *all of which need to be taken*. (The reader will note that this list is slightly different from the eight points in Chapter Six under "How Do You Create Psychological Safety?" to reflect the priorities in Alpha. Involvement of the learners was mentioned throughout as a separate point.)

- A *compelling positive vision*: If I learn this new stuff, how will we all be better off?
- *Formal training*: What is involved in the new behavior and attitudes? That is, what are the laws, what are the dangerous substances, what are the procedures for dealing with them, whom do I call for what, etc.?
- *Informal training*: getting the know-how and skill of handling the new and possibly ambiguous situations (is that oil on the water, or some other substance?); learning new standards by which things are to be judged.
- A *practice field and coaches*: Can I try my hand in situations where mistakes are OK and I can learn from them? Will there be coaches around to tell me whether I am doing OK and how to do better?
- *Corrective feedback*: If I take some action, will someone tell me whether I did it right or wrong? If I am doing it right, will I be told and rewarded?
- A *reward and discipline system consistent with the new learning*: If I or others do it right, will we get consistent rewards? If I or others are failing in some way, will we get appropriate feedback? If others are

Exhibit 7.1 Excerpts of Notes Presented to "Alpha Power" Change Committee (*continued*)

violating the new rules, will I see them being appropriately disciplined?

- *Positive role models and examples as well as examples and cases of what not to do*: Will we observe our own managers all the way up the line walking the talk and setting positive examples?
- *Support groups*: groups in which learning problems can be aired and in which I can become involved in helping to design my own learning process.

(*text continued from page 151*)

- You keep information about violations in the group and fix the problem within the group.
- You do not "rat out" a buddy who may be overlooking or ignoring an environmental problem; you do not report him or her, nor do you even confront the person if a safety or environmental procedure is violated.
- You punish fellow employees who have informed on the group (that is, called the court-appointed monitor on the private hot line).
- Technical expertise and seniority are the keys to advancement.
- The company takes care of you if you are a long-service employee, even if your technical skills have atrophied.
- Good work is taken for granted and automatically recognized; one does not have to advertise or brag about one's accomplishments.

The two major themes that emerge from this cultural profile are, first, that the whole system works because of a strong hierarchy and strong in-group loyalty and, second, that both management and employees share an engineering mentality in which attention is focused on fixing technical problems efficiently without worrying about how the public, the government, and other outside stakeholders might perceive the company and its behavior. For example, because of extensive underground cables the company can only locate a certain percentage of leaks of dielectric fluids, which potentially contaminate the environment. In presentations about these efforts, all the energy is focused on the sophisticated way in which they recover 80 percent of the leaked fluids. That the other 20 percent—which amounts to 20,000 gallons per year—cannot be located and dealt with is more or less ignored as a public relations problem in spite of the fact that this might still seem like a very large amount to the public.

It is these elements of the culture that I found hardest to deal with, especially those that involved group norms to keep things in the work unit, respect fellow employees' independence even if they are violating EH&S rules, and accept hierarchical authority even if it means violating EH&S rules. The only way I could see to accomplish change in this area was by involving all echelons of the organization, especially the employees themselves. If they did not participate actively in defining the methods of learning, their norms would not change.

Structural and Process Interventions

It was recognized that the culture of Alpha Power did indeed have elements that would need to change, but it was also recognized that the elements of the culture that were built around strong hierarchy, deference to superiors, paternalism, and an implicit promise of lifetime employment could aid in getting the EH&S message out. The company made a number of structural and process changes that reflected these existing cultural elements:

- A senior VP for environmental affairs was hired.
- Environmental managers were placed in each operating unit and given authority to determine how EH&S-related work was to be performed.

- Detailed procedures for identifying and remediating environmental hazards were developed and published.
- Intensive training programs on these procedures for supervisors and employees were launched.
- Strong disciplinary procedures were instituted to punish supervisors or fellow employees who harassed anyone reporting to the court-appointed monitor.
- Public recognition and awards were given to employees who demonstrated environmental responsibility and invented new procedures for heightening both efficiency and environmental responsibility.
- New technologies were created to aid in dealing with oil spills and other problems.
- Detailed measurement systems were instituted to track the rate of environmental incidents.
- The oversight committees met regularly to monitor the whole program.
- The auditing department investigated all EH&S incidents to determine root cause and other causal factors, and to build a database from which generalizations about EH&S issues could be made.

Creation of the Culture Committee

In addition to these measures, I suggested that it was essential to involve the next layer of management. The VP of environmental affairs (my primary client) and I decided to form a culture committee comprising all of the next layer of officers from the key line and staff organizations. This committee was also given the culture presentation and invited, over the course of the next several monthly meetings, to wrestle with the question of how to involve the unionized employees in the total transformation process.

It was my assumption that unless this layer of the organization changed its signals as to what was important, the message would not mean much at the first-line supervisory and employee level, no matter how loudly executive management proclaimed its new values. It was essential to do this in a group so that managers could learn from each other and gradually change their own norms as a prerequisite to sending new signals down into the organization beneath them. The first task of this group was to translate the company's vision around the values of teamwork, openness, and responsibility into a concrete new way of thinking and working for employees.

Defining the New Way of Thinking and Working

The VP and I functioned as cochairs of the culture committee. We decided to introduce the formal task of specifying what the employee attitudes, thought processes, and behavior in the ideal future company would look like. What did it mean to be an open, responsible, team-oriented employee?

To illustrate: in the old way of working, if a hospital transformer broke down and the work crew dispatched to fix it discovered that their truck was leaking oil into a nearby sewer, there was no question that they would fix the transformer first and then worry about the oil spill later. In the new way of working, they were required to do both, something that seemed impossible. To give another example, in the old way of working if one member of a work crew was not wearing safety equipment or was doing something unsafe, crewmates would say nothing, even if it endangered them. In the new way of working, they were supposed to be mutually responsible and monitor each other, something that seemed equally impossible given the group norms.

My group interviews with the environmental managers and EH&S consultants who worked in the field led me to conclude that the goals were clear but that no one in the hierarchy had solutions. The solutions would have to come from the workgroups themselves once they accepted the goals as valid. They would figure out how to integrate, or at least align, productivity and environmental concerns. In other words, the role of senior management was to clarify that the vision had to be implemented, but *how* it was implemented depended on the involvement of the employees. Empowerment needed to be real in sharing with the employees the responsibility for coming up with solutions. As such solutions were invented, the individuals and teams who made the inventions could be highly publicized, rewarded, and made into role models for other parts of Alpha.

The Time Out Program. One such solution, invented in a geographical subunit of Alpha, was called the Time Out Program. Each employee was issued a small green card with instructions to call time out whenever he or she felt that to proceed would involve some EH&S risk. The job would then have to be stopped until an EH&S expert could assess the situation and give directions on what to do next. Needless to say, considerable anxiety developed in the management ranks because of the possibility that employees would use Time Out frivolously or irresponsibly, but that has not happened. In those cases where an employee did stop a job it was found that expert help was indeed needed, and new procedures were instituted. The program was so successful in this one unit that the company eventually made it a general program throughout and gave it senior management's blessing and support.

Notice that Time Out is a concrete way of changing the hierarchical norms of the culture by giving employees the license to stop a job, which means refusing to continue to do what their supervisor had sanctioned or even explicitly ordered. Notice also that the old norm of always following orders is now undermined, but the new norm of "we have the power and the responsibility to stop a job when necessary" is not yet totally accepted. A new culture has not formed; only new behavior has been sanctioned. Forming a new cultural element depends on whether the new behavior is, in the long run, successful in making the company more responsible and productive. In the meantime, acceptance of this program by supervisors is a clear signal that the old hierarchical culture is gradually evolving toward employee empowerment around EH&S issues.

Employee involvement in safety committees. The new way of working was getting clearer in the environmental area, but it remained a problem in the safety area because of the norm of not ratting out or confronting your buddies. The vision was clear: good safety requires teamwork, and it is the responsibility of every member of the team to be sure every other member is following safety procedures. If one member is not wearing a safety helmet or safety glasses, it is the *responsibility* of the other team members to point this out and demand compliance. But this means abandoning the implicit heroic model of getting the job done through individual heroic behavior, as well as abandoning the norm that each employee has autonomy in deciding what to wear or not wear.

To deal with this dilemma, it is again necessary to look for creative examples within the organization. One came from a department in which the labor management safety committee decided that safety inspections and postaccident reviews should not be done solely by safety experts but rather by employees who were peers in rank. If a fellow employee from another group points out to a given workgroup the "stupidity" of not wearing safety equipment, this clearly has more impact than if the message comes from the supervisor or a staff expert. More mutual responsibility has been obtained in this department, but it remains to be seen whether this peer group process will be accepted in other parts of Alpha.

Employee involvement in equipment redesign. Another example comes from a group in which some engineers found that the safety equipment was cumbersome and uncomfortable. Instead of the traditional approach of "training" employees to use the existing equipment, they launched an employee group to redesign the equipment with the specific goal of making it usable in the particular working conditions they typically face. Again, if this process of redesign by employees themselves proves to be successful and widespread, the culture changes further. But this is often a slow process of invention, diffusion, and acceptance, and even then it does not produce a new culture unless it is followed by success.

Employee involvement in planning work. Finally, what of the hospital transformer and oil spill? The environmental affairs representatives working with employees pointed out that the solution, which they had adopted, lay in better planning for all environmental contingencies. If you know that trucks leak, then carry extra blankets and buckets of sand. It takes only ten seconds to contain the spill; then you fix the transformer, and after that you clean up the spill. But to learn to plan is itself countercultural if heroic fire fighting is the norm, so it remains to be seen whether education, training, positive role models. and recognition-and-reward systems are sufficient to change this norm. In any case, without employee involvement it is unlikely that such norms will change.

In summary, the new way of thinking and working involves using elements of the culture that aid the change process and confronting elements that stand in the way. To change elements involves all of the steps in the earlier section on overcoming learning anxiety (Chapter Six, "How Do You Create Psychological Safety?") and often hinges on deep involvement of the employees who most feel the impact of the change. Especially if employee norms are involved, they cannot be changed by managerial fiat. Only the group can decide to abandon a given norm and begin to think along different lines. The job of the change agent is to continue to invent and implement processes that facilitate new ideas, ensure that the ideas circulate, make certain that all levels of management and employees are appropriately involved in inventing solutions, and keep educating management to the realities of what is ultimately involved in transformative change processes.

Lessons

Alpha Power illustrates the complexity of deciding what needs to change. Clearly, the company had to become environmentally responsible to be freed from probation, but it was not easy to translate this general requirement into specific daily behaviors. At the same time, senior management wanted to inculcate or reinforce some new values: openness, teamwork, individual sense of responsibility, and better planning. These values are ambiguous in terms of what new behavior is required. It is only when the organization is specific about "not lying to the government," "reporting all environmental events immediately," "checking out one another on safety equipment use," and so on that culture surfaces as both an aid and a constraint. It is at this point that the new behavior is recognized as involving a whole new way of thinking as well.

A major education program on what culture dynamics were all about had to be launched prior to figuring out which cultural interventions to make. This educational process had to filter down through the echelons of the organization so that the new managerial signals of what would be rewarded and punished were consistent and in line with the new values. When it came to trying to change cultural norms at the employee level, it was necessary to look for innovative solutions among the employees themselves.

The Alpha Power program is just beginning. Whether and how fast the culture actually changes depends on the degree of success of the innovations in making Alpha a more productive and responsible organization.

Practical Implication

You must create a steering committee that designs its own transformative change process based on your industry, your company, your particular culture, and the specific change problem you face. What you should draw out of the Alpha case is the insight that a change program has to be tailored to the specific situation. General principles such as those outlined in the Alpha memo (Exhibit 7.1) apply, but how they are implemented varies from one project to another.

A second insight is that the devil is in the details. How the general principles are implemented at the level of detailed changes in work procedures determines the success or failure of your ultimate program. Don't let a culture consultant sell you on a standardized program of diagnosis and intervention. Bring in a process consultant who can help you figure out your own program and help you implement the interventions that you yourself choose.

Case Example: Moderate Culture Change in Ciba-Geigy

Ciba-Geigy (C-G) illustrates well a case where culture mostly aided a turnaround process that was necessitated by economic and technological forces.The chemical sector had overcapacity and needed to be downsized, while the pharmaceutical sector needed to become much more profitable relative to its competitors. As mentioned before, the geographical units and divisions had already become lean, but Basel headquarters had not gotten rid of much of its overhead; the line units were pressuring headquarters for this to happen.

The situation was defined as a "turnaround." A task force of senior managers functioning as a steering committee decided on twenty-five separate projects that would have to be done to achieve the vision of what the C-G of the future had to be. Small groups of senior executives then went to each of the units, explaining in detail what had to be done, and offering resources. At these meetings, the vision of the future ideal state was communicated. The personal presence of senior executives made it clear that the goals were nonnegotiable. This was to be a serious turnaround. Each project had a manager and linkage to a board member who monitored and oversaw the project. The steering committee met monthly to track progress and intervene where necessary. A three-year timetable was mandated for the changes to occur.

Each project group then had to design its own transformative change process to meet its objectives within the three-year time frame. For example, in the chemical division a major downsizing process had to be implemented. One of the change team's important insights was that not only would they let people go in a dignified way (reflecting C-G values) but special attention would be paid to the motivation and morale of those employees and managers who remained in the division. There would be guilt feelings relative to their friends who lost their jobs, and survival anxiety in terms of their own career. Special programs were designed to deal with both of these feelings.

In the pharmaceutical division, on the other hand, a major program in marketing and financial management was to be launched. Managerial thinking had to move from the assumption that R&D would always guarantee enough new drugs to enable the division to grow, to the assumption that in the future there would be very few new drugs so the emphasis had to shift to more competitive selling and tighter cost controls to protect profit margins.

Did Culture Change?

In all of the projects, there was much talk of culture change, but in fact the C-G program was a clear case of identifying a set of business problems and using the best elements of the existing culture to solve them. Ciba-Geigy enlisted its authority system, hierarchy, predilection for using groups and teams, and traditions of loyalty and subordination to make major changes in each unit. For example, in the chemical division and at Basel headquarters, the positive cultural assumption that "we treat our people well" led to a very sensitive, carefully designed layoff process in which each person was talked to by the boss and senior management and given a full explanation of what had to be done and why. Supplementing this personal explanation, C-G created a program of maximizing reduction through attrition, extensive career counseling to help people find new jobs, opportunities for transitional consulting or part-time work, generous severance packages, and generous early retirement programs. In the end, C-G managers felt they had affirmed their culture rather than changed it; yet they solved their business problems.

Lessons

Changing business practices, reducing costs, rightsizing, etc. do not necessarily involve culture change. Rather, this case illustrates the importance of focusing on the business problems and using the existing culture to change whatever needs changing. Only if the changes have an impact on the existing culture, as in the case of Alpha Power, does culture change become an issue.

Practical Implication

At this point, I want to remind you that not all transformative change is necessarily culture change. This is important because the culture can often be used in support of a specific desired change in business practices. Review in your own mind some of the changes your company needs, and ask yourself how much they actually require culture change.

Organizational Midlife Crisis and Potential Decline

Continued success creates strongly held shared assumptions, and thus a strong culture. If the internal and external environments remain stable, this is an advantage. However, if there is a change in the environment, some of those shared assumptions can become liabilities, precisely because of their strength. This stage is sometimes reached when the organization is no longer able to grow because it has saturated its markets or its products have become obsolete. These developments are not necessarily correlated with age, size, or number of managerial generations, but rather reflect the interaction between the organization's outputs and the environmental opportunities and constraints.

Age does matter, however, if culture change is required. If an organization has a long history of success with certain assumptions about itself and the environment, it is unlikely to want to challenge or reexamine them. Even if they are brought to consciousness, the members of the organization are likely to want to hold on to them because they justify the past and are the source of pride and self-esteem. Such assumptions now operate as filters making it difficult for key managers to understand alternative strategies for survival and renewal (Donaldson and Lorsch, 1983).

Outside consultants can be brought in and clear alternatives identified. But no matter how clear and persuasive the consultant tries to be, some alternatives are not even understood if they do not fit the old culture, and some are resisted, even if understood, because they create too much survival anxiety or guilt, or because there is insufficient psychological safety. No matter how much insight top management has, some new assumptions cannot be implemented down the line in the organization because people simply do not comprehend or accept what the new strategy requires.

As previously cited, a vivid example in DEC was its inability to develop a product to compete effectively with the PC. All of senior management recognized that DEC should be in the PC market, but they tacitly assumed that the sophisticated user was their prime target; this led to building three versions of the PC, all of them too elegant, too expensive, and still too complicated to use. The engineers were completely embedded in their traditional assumptions about the nature of computers and the marketplace. They believed they were designing a truly competitive product and were surprised that all three versions failed in the marketplace.

In a situation where growth has slowed and decline is imminent, the basic choices are between (1) rapidly transforming parts of the culture to permit the organization to become adaptive once again through some kind of turnaround, or (2) destroying the organization and its culture through a process of total reorganization via merger, acquisition, or bankruptcy proceedings. In either case, strong new change managers or transformational leaders are likely to be needed to unfreeze the organization and launch the change programs (Kotter and Heskett, 1992; Tichy and Devanna, 1986). In either case, the human cost is high as the new managers discover that changing cultural assumptions is often accomplished most quickly by simply getting rid of the people who are the carriers of the old assumptions. At this stage, cultural transformation can only be accomplished by a drastic change program, the subject of the next section.

Drastic Culture Change

If the change process outlined in the previous section "Planned and Managed Culture Change" does not produce the business results that are needed in terms of the ideal future state, change leaders seek more drastic measures. The most common of these is to bring in an outside CEO who has a different set of values and assumptions from those of the present culture. If a hybrid manager can be found in a subculture, he or she can serve that function. The board typically empowers the new CEO to produce a major turnaround—and explicitly or implicitly states how long he or she has to produce better business results. The extreme version of this process is to bring in a known turnaround manager (for example, Al Dunlap), who promises to bring the company back into some kind of financial health by immediately taking whatever measures are necessary. More measured versions of this process are exemplified by General Electric empowering Jack Welch, IBM bringing in Lou Gerstner, or Kodak selecting George Fisher. In between is a case like that of DEC with Robert Palmer, which we review next.

If the new turnaround manager sees major barriers in the present culture, it is inevitable that under time pressure a period of cultural destruction has to take place. Many managers have to evolve new ways of thinking and behaving very rapidly, or they are forced out of the organization. In some instances (perhaps GE is a good example), a strong and charismatic leader can produce change in the existing cadre of executives. But as the case below shows, the existing cadre often clings to the old culture that has made them successful and therefore has to be replaced before the business problems begin to be solved. We should have no illusions, therefore, about the possibility of major cultural transformation without massive human costs. For old cultural assumptions to be destroyed, the organization has to convert or get rid of the culture carriers.

Case Example: Massive Cultural Change and Destruction

For a variety of reasons, during the 1980s DEC became slow and inefficient. Competition was stiffer, market windows were narrower, and DEC's cost structure was out of line with those of its competitors. A number of downsizing efforts were attempted, but they did not, in the board's estimation, go far enough to make DEC viable and profitable. The culture was perceived to be too egalitarian and the decision process too slow. The subunits had become too powerful and unwilling to integrate around any kind of central strategy. Conflict over strategic goals and the means to be used to achieve anything were rampant. The choice of Robert Palmer to succeed Ken Olsen appeared to be motivated by bringing in someone who understood DEC, having spent part of his career there, but who would be much more disciplined in his approach to fixing DEC's problems. This change is an example of bringing in a hybrid manager from a subculture built on very different assumptions and charging him with creating a major turnaround.

The major changes instituted by Palmer over a period of several years were to centralize decision making, tighten discipline, shed unproductive units, and, most important, get rid of most of the carriers of the old culture. Some were fired, some retired, and many left because they could not work under the new regime. All agreed that the old DEC culture was being destroyed in favor of a more traditional autocratic and disciplined hierarchy. In their place, Palmer brought in a variety of outsiders with different experience, skills, and basic assumptions about how to run an organization. Employees who remained in DEC frequently lamented the destruction of the old culture, and many of them left to start new enterprises that would recapture the old culture. For many, the attachment to the old culture is so strong that they formed an "alumni association," created a newsletter to stay in touch with each other, and have regular reunions. Those who went to other companies attempted to institute some of the principles they felt had worked well in DEC. Paradoxically, even though the DEC culture within DEC was largely destroyed, as a set of concepts of how to run a company that same culture survived among various ex-DEC employees.

The important point to note in this case is that the culture change could not be accomplished with the present set of players at the senior level. They were too embedded in the old way of working since it had led to DEC's success in the first place. To institute a new way of working, Palmer had to recruit another set of senior-management players. Whether this created a new culture or simply started DEC down a path of more transitions and changes is not clear, but it is obvious that DEC became profitable enough to become an attractive target of acquisition for Compaq. What further changes in ways of working this will bring remains to be seen. It is also not clear whether Compaq's culture is similar in certain respects to the old DEC culture or whether, as a result of the acquisition, the DEC culture will be even further eroded and replaced.

Lessons

The major lesson of the DEC experience is that you cannot change core cultural assumptions without removing the carriers of those cultural assumptions. Culture destruction is a painful and brutal process in human terms. It is also clear, from the degree to which ex-DEC employees have held on to the cultural values that they grew up with, that "the culture" was not destroyed in the heads of the people—only in the DEC organization as such.

A second lesson comes from observations of failed turnarounds. The new outside leader must become familiar enough with the old culture to understand just what needs to be changed and what kind of resistance will be encountered. The hybrid outsiders are in a much better position to figure this out. As I mentioned in the case of Jones Food (Chapter Five), when severe crises followed the founder's death and his lieutenant's retirement, the company attempted to bring in strong outsiders; but the existing culture of this family firm was so strong that the first three failed. Only when the family brought in a person who had been in Jones Food before and who was recruited back after a period of independent success did they find someone who could manage the necessary culture change.

The story of Apple is somewhat similar in that John Sculley and then Gilbert Amelio were evidently not able to bring about some of the changes the company needed, so the board went back to Steve Jobs—who clearly understood the culture, having been one of its founders and architects. Welch's success in GE is undoubtedly related to his having grown up the company, and Gerstner's success in IBM is probably related to the fact that he was bringing back some of the marketing values that had so badly eroded.

Practical Implication

The level of transformation in turnarounds of this kind has an organizational and financial logic all its own. It is unlikely that you can influence the dynamic very much from the point of view of planned change. If your organization finds itself in enough trouble to seek outside leadership, you must plan for a period of painful human dislocation. As in the Ciba-Geigy turnaround, pay special attention to the morale and motivation of the survivors.

The Bottom Line

This chapter has highlighted the most difficult aspects of organizational transformation and culture change. We have focused on the mature organization, where change is not evolution or new learning but first and foremost unlearning and predictable resistance to change. People do not cling so tightly to the culture in a mature organization as they do in a young and growing one, but the mature company is harder to change because the culture has become more embedded in its structures and routines. If enough disconfirmation is present and executive leadership decides major changes are needed in how the organization is working, a planned, managed change process can be launched. Such a process requires creating a change team to function as a steering committee and become for a time a parallel system, in order to gain a more objective view of the culture.

The steering committee is not only the place where the new way of thinking and behaving can be conceptualized but also where the old culture can be assessed in terms of where it aids or hinders the needed changes in business processes. The actual change program that is launched reflects the particular culture of the organization doing the change. It must be congruent with the general change model presented in Chapter Six, but the details of how this is done depend on the particulars of that organization's culture. The cases of Alpha Power and Ciba-Geigy are examples of two such managed change programs.

If many elements of the culture are dysfunctional, executive management may decide on a more drastic change program involving a turnaround manager as the new CEO, brought in from the outside. But this is risky if he or she does not understand the present culture. A successful turnaround is more likely if the new CEO is a hybrid manager who has some familiarity with the present culture because of past membership or association with it. If the CEO is charismatic, he or she may be able to convert many of the present managers of the organization. More probably, the new CEO has to get rid of the major culture carriers and replace them with new people whose assumptions better fit the current realities that the organization faces. The case of DEC is an illustration of this scenario.

As a final point, I note that both planned change and turnarounds are likely to be painful, involve removal of many people, take many years to accomplish, and only institute a new way of thinking and working whose eventual success is still not guaranteed. If they are successful, the beginnings of a new culture are launched; but only with repeated success do the new ways of thinking and working become a new culture in its own right.

Chapter Eight

When Cultures Meet

Acquisitions, Mergers, Joint Ventures, and Other Blended Organizations

- Why Not Do a Formal Cultural Assessment Prior to Moving Ahead?
- Culture Traps (The Illusion That We Understand One Another)
- The Need for Dialogue at Cultural Boundaries
- Introducing Dialogue into Cross-Cultural Assessment
- The Bottom Line

Cultures meet anytime there is a merger of two companies, when one company acquires another, or when two companies engage in a joint venture. A merger attempts to blend two cultures, without necessarily treating one or the other as dominant. In acquisition, the acquired organization automatically becomes a subculture in the larger culture of the acquiring company. In the joint venture the new organization must start with bringing two cultures together from scratch. In each case, the problem of blending or assimilation is compounded by the fact that the total, new unit does not have any shared history, so one or the other subunit probably feels inferior, threatened, angry, and defensive (Buono and Bowditch, 1989; Centre for Organization Studies, 1990; McManus and Hergert, 1988).

The more overt characteristics of organizations—such as shared or compatible technologies, shared business goals, financial compatibility, common markets, and product synergy—usually drive this process. It is often overlooked until too late that the means by which the goals are accomplished in the two organizations may be very different, and the underlying assumptions about business and human processes may actually conflict with one another. Rarely checked are those aspects that might be considered "cultural": the philosophy or style of the company; technological origins, which might provide clues as to basic assumptions; beliefs about its mission and future; and how it organizes itself internally. Yet a cultural mismatch in an acquisition, merger, or joint venture is as great a risk as a financial, product, or market mismatch.

Some concrete examples will make this point clear. Some years ago, General Foods (GF) purchased Burgerchef, a successful chain of hamburger restaurants. But despite ten years of concerted effort, the parent could not make the acquisition profitable. First of all, GF did not anticipate that many of the best Burgerchef managers would leave because they did not like GF's management philosophy. Then, instead of hiring new managers with experience in the fast-food business, GF assigned some of its own managers to run the new business. This was its second mistake, since these managers did not understand the technology of the fast-food business and hence were unable to use many of the marketing techniques that had proved effective in GF. Third, GF imposed on Burgerchef many of the control systems and procedures that had historically proved useful for GF, not realizing that this would drive the operating costs of the chain too high. GF's managers never completely understood franchise operations and hence could not get a feel for what it would take to run that kind of business profitably. Eventually GF sold Burgerchef, having lost many millions of dollars over a decade. With hindsight, it was clear that GF never understood that a fast-food business creates a very different kind of culture than a packaged-food business does.

Lack of understanding of the cultural risks of buying a franchised business was brought out even more clearly in another case. United Fruit, at the time a stuffy, traditional, moralistic company whose management prided itself on high ethical standards, bought a chain of fast-food restaurants that were locally franchised all around the country. The company's managers discovered, much to their chagrin, that one of the biggest of these restaurants and its associated motel was the local brothel. The activities of the town were so well integrated around this restaurant/motel that the alternative of closing it down posed the risk of drawing precisely the kind of attention United Fruit wanted at all costs to avoid. The managers asked themselves, after the fact, "Should we have known what our acquisition involved on this not-very-obvious level? Should we have understood our own value system better, to ensure compatibility?"

A third example highlighting the clash of two sets of assumptions about authority is the case of the two first-generation high-tech companies in Chapter One, which we called Company A and Company B. Company A, run by a founder who injected strong beliefs that one succeeds by stimulating initiative and egalitarianism, was bought by Company B, this one run by a strongly autocratic entrepreneur who trained his employees to be highly disciplined and formal. The purchasing company wanted and needed the acquiree's managerial talent, but within one year of the deal most of the best managers from Company A had left because they could not adapt to the formal autocratic style of Company B. The autocratic entrepreneur could not understand why this happened and had no sensitivity to the cultural differences between the two companies.

What is striking in these cases is the lack of insight on the part of the acquiring company into *its own* organizational culture, its unconscious assumptions about how a business should be run. Contemplating some recent major mergers (such as Citicorp and Travelers, AMOCO and British Petroleum, Chrysler and Daimler Benz, NYNEX and Bell Atlantic), one can only wonder how these corporate giants will mesh not only their businesses but also their cultures. The histories of these companies suggest that substantial cultural differences almost certainly exist between them.

The joint ventures that are springing up all over the globe involve not only different corporate cultures but even different national cultures. When two cultures meet, the basic problem is that more than one culture must be aligned, reconciled, merged, or absorbed. In Chapter One, I pointed out that there are only three logically distinct possibilities: the cultures can remain independent of each other and coexist, one culture can gradually dominate and ultimately absorb the other culture, or the two cultures can blend into a new culture that draws on both. When you read about mergers, acquisitions, and joint ventures, there is usually a lot of rhetoric about benchmarking the cultures against each other and picking the best of both (alternative three). But this is rarely achieved because usually neither partner takes culture seriously enough to really figure out where the synergies are and how to take advantage of them. Culture is recognized as an issue, but rarely is it analyzed or assessed to a sufficient degree to actually locate synergies or conflicts.

Salk (1992) made detailed observations of three joint ventures in which the parent companies came from different countries: a Canadian-Italian joint venture based in Europe, a French-German joint venture based in France, and a German-U.S. joint venture based in the United States. The culture issues played themselves out in three distinct ways. In the first case, the Canadian company espoused cultural equality, but for "practical reasons" the physical location was near the Canadian parent's European headquarters, which led to many of the office procedures being adopted from what headquarters was doing. Early interactions led to mutually negative stereotypes—and they still dominated interaction three years later. The Canadians liked to write things down and make requests on paper. The Italians felt things on paper were unimportant and if something was to be done one had to go ask for it in person; therefore they tended to ignore memos, which led the Canadians to conclude that the Italians were unmotivated and uncooperative. The Italian parent company functioned in terms of personal relationships and personal influence; the Canadian parent favored formal roles, job descriptions, and procedures. This led the Italians to view the Canadians as hopelessly bureaucratic.

The significant point is that each side felt it inappropriate to bring their feelings out into the open. Somehow, at this level culture became undiscussable because to do so risked losing face. So the group lived with its stereotypes, grumbled silently to the researcher in interviews, but did nothing to correct the situation. So far, business results have not forced the issue because of a favorable business climate; but if that changes, the organization will have to confront more directly the cultural gap they are living with.

In the German-French venture, the direction of cultural domination is increasingly being determined by the actual ratio of French and German managers in the venture and the location of the business. In this case, the Germans appear to be adapting to the French style because the joint venture is located in France.

In the U.S.-German case, the situation is more complicated. Each parent decided to provide cross-cultural training on what the other culture was like, and the venture budgeted for a one-week outward-bound-type experience to help the two teams come together. The initial company training created strong stereotypes, and the joint training was unfortunately canceled for reasons of time and money. The early interactions were very much dominated by the learned stereotypes. This showed up, for example, in trying to set production targets; the Germans assumed that the U.S. numbers were always inflated since "Americans always expect budgets and targets to be cut by higher management." On the other hand, the Americans were warned that Germans are always too conservative. Each side tried to give fairly accurate numbers but totally mistrusted the numbers from the other group; again, they were unable to bring this out into the open lest they offend each other. So each group would complain to the researcher but argue that things could not be brought up in meetings.

In this last case, some cultural blending eventually resulted from a business crisis. Production was well below what either group had predicted, there were unanticipated labor problems, and the U.S. parent changed key managers after these problems arose. To fix the problems, the two nationalities finally got together as a single group and chose procedures on the basis of which cultural assumptions were best suited to solving the new external problem. In the labor relations area, the Germans ended up leaning more on the Americans, but in the technical area the reverse happened; gradually, a new way of working was forged by taking some assumptions from each parent.

Salk makes the point that although these were cross-national joint ventures, another decisive factor determining outcomes was the specific parent company's policy regarding career development. If the career track was seen as still located in the parent, it was much harder for the venture to become a team. This situation was especially problematic in the Italian case since those managers had a much higher incentive to keep their relationships to the parent in good order than to learn to get along with the Canadians. What Salk initially defined to be a study across *national* cultural boundaries turned out to be as much a study of corporate cultures and their career development policies.

Why Not Do a Formal Cultural Assessment Prior to Moving Ahead?

Serious formal cultural assessment along the lines of Chapter Four is usually not possible because the negotiations leading up to the merger or joint venture have to be kept secret. But this creates the danger that you do not discover important differences until after the parties commit themselves to the new organization. Recall Ciba-Geigy's acquisition of Airwick and its subsequent discovery that it could not stand to be associated with Airwick's products and processes—even though they were making money.

However, once a merger or joint venture is publicly announced, it would make complete sense to engage in such formal assessment. The two organizations could form a series of task forces with equal numbers of participants from each cultural unit. These task forces should then assess the artifacts, espoused values, and shared tacit assumptions in the main areas of mission, goals, means, measurement, corrective mechanisms, language, group boundaries, and status and reward systems. In fact, one should do such an assessment within an organization that is planning acquisitions, mergers, and joint ventures as part of its own preparation for such activities. The organization should know as much about *its own* culture as possible.

Practical Implications

Self-assessment. If your organization is planning or implementing a merger, acquisition or joint venture, start a cultural self-assessment process as soon as possible. Ask yourself especially what the core shared assumptions and values are that you would not be willing to compromise; use these insights as a diagnostic in looking at potential partners. Set up a straw-man organization with which to merge, to provide a business reason for doing the culture self-assessment.

Cross-culture assessment. Create a set of task forces, one-half from each culture, and assign them various content areas of the culture. Use Exhibit 3.1 (page 30) as a guideline. Have the members of the task force visit one another's organizations to develop a feeling firsthand for the other culture.

Culture Traps (The Illusion That We Understand One Another)

When the externals such as products and markets fit, it is very tempting to assume that people of goodwill will figure each other out and make the necessary accommodations to work together. To show goodwill, we tend to exaggerate the degree to which we actually understand each other.

One reason we exaggerate the degree of mutual understanding is to avoid the pain of being "unknown." If I am asked to work with someone from another organization and he or she has never worked with me, it is painful to realize that I have to establish my identity from scratch. It is less painful to assume that we are probably basically alike and proceed from there.

Only later might we suddenly discover great differences in how we operate. At that point, a second trap is usually sprung: the need to cling to and justify my own way of doing things. Suddenly my way seems to make complete sense and I cannot for the life of me figure out why the "other" wants to do things differently. I am likely at this point to go into a persuasion mode and to stereotype others as not making sense if they don't agree with me.

This springs the third trap in cross-cultural communication: our disagreement and our stereotype are themselves undiscussable. We have no way of backing off and examining our assumptions without risking offending the other person or demeaning ourselves.

In the rest of this chapter, I treat all of these forms of intercultural traps as having basically the same characteristic, though, of course, the details of how things work out are highly specific. But from a cultural point of view, there are only a few basic points that must be remembered, and it is these I concentrate on. The key to cross-cultural understanding is *dialogue*.

The Need for Dialogue at Cultural Boundaries

If we take culture seriously, we will realize that two cultures trying to meet constructively have to go beyond the kind of assessment I have described so far because they do not know whether they are even using the same meanings for seemingly shared concepts. The meaning that Ciba-Geigy attached to Airwick products could not have been foreseen. General Foods could not have obtained a feel for what it takes to run a fast-food hamburger chain through formal cultural assessment. To reap cultural insights at this level requires either participating in each other's cultures by actually sending employees into the other organization for some period of time, or creating dialogues between members of the two cultures that allow differing assumptions to surface. Assuming that exchange of employees may be impractical, I will focus on how to create such dialogues.

Dialogue is a form of conversation that allows the participants to relax sufficiently to begin examining the assumptions that lie behind their thought processes (Isaacs, 1993; Isaacs, 1999; Schein, 1993). Instead of trying to solve problems rapidly, the dialogue process attempts to slow down the conversation to allow participants to reflect on what comes out of their own mouths and what they hear from the mouths of others. The key to initiating dialogic conversation is to create a setting in which participants feel secure enough to suspend their need to win arguments, clarify everything they say, and challenge each other every time they disagree. Dialogue is more a low-key "talking around the campfire," allowing enough time for and encouraging reflective conversation, rather than confrontational conversation. But its purpose is not just to have a quiet, reflective conversation; rather, it is to allow participants to begin to see where their deeper levels of thought and tacit assumptions differ.

Introducing Dialogue into Cross-Cultural Assessment

If a joint venture, partnership, merger, or acquisition is at the stage where the participants can be revealed to each other and to the public, the planners should create focused dialogues around the major elements of the strategy, goals, and means to be used in the new organization. Operationally, this means:

- Creating a series of task forces whose membership is from both cultures
- Asking the new intercultural groups to explore major areas of how each organization operates

- Training each task force to use dialogue as the major vehicle for their conversation

The basic presumption is that the normal assessment process referred to above—just comparing artifacts and espoused values around various business processes—does not reveal enough about the shared, tacit, underlying assumptions, though such comparison of artifacts can be a good start for the dialogue. As differences in structure and procedures are identified, the crucial next step is to explore *reflectively* what the underlying assumptions are that create the overt differences. The key to this reflective process is to examine your own assumptions first; only when they are more or less understood can you try to appreciate the assumptions of the others. For this to work, all of the parties to the dialogue have to be willing to suspend impulses to disagree, challenge, clarify, and elaborate. By slowing down the conversation, we learn to hear the deeper layers of our own discourse and realize how much our perceptions, thoughts, and feelings are based on learned assumptions. We begin to experience our own culture, that is, the degree to which our own group identifications and backgrounds color our thought processes. As we discover this in ourselves, we are readier to hear it and accept it in others.

Practical Implication

If you are trying to gain mutual understanding between two cultures, you must create a dialogue form of conversation. You can act as the facilitator, or if you bring in a dialogue facilitator, you should set the scene:

1. Select ten to twenty people who represent the two cultures equally.
2. Seat everyone in a circle, or as near to it as possible.

3. Lay out the purpose of the dialogue: "to be able to listen more reflectively to ourselves and to each other, to get a sense of the similarities and differences in our cultures."

4. Start the conversation by having the members in turn check in by introducing who they are and what goals they have for the meeting.

5. After everyone has checked in, the facilitator should launch a very general question, such as, "What was it like to come into this company?" Everyone in the circle should, in turn, answer the question for his or her company with the ground rule that there be no interruptions or questions until everyone has given an answer.

6. Encourage an open conversation on what everyone has just heard without the constraints of proceeding in order or having to withhold questions and comments.

7. If the topic runs dry or the group loses energy, introduce another question, for example, "How are decisions made in this organization?" Again, have everyone in turn give an answer before general conversation begins.

8. Let the differences emerge naturally; don't try to make general statements, because the purpose is mutual understanding, not necessarily clear description.

9. After a couple of hours, ask the group to poll itself by asking each person in turn to share one or two insights about either his or her own culture or the other one; these can be written down.

10. Depending on time available, continue the process, or plan another meeting, or do the same thing with another group.

The Bottom Line

The cultural dynamics involved in mergers, acquisitions, and joint ventures are fundamentally different from the culture evolution and change dynamics we have covered before because mature cultures are coming together. Ideally we look for blending, by which the new organization takes the most functional elements of each culture. But this presumes ability to decipher the cultures, which is rarely present until long after the new organization has been formed. In fact, when mature cultures meet, the members of both cultures are trapped in the illusion that they understand each other better than they do, and caught up as well in the face-saving necessity of not challenging each other too severely.

In preparing for a new organization, it is essential that at the least the members of each organization have maximum insight into their own culture. A useful exercise for any organization contemplating merger or joint venture is to set up a hypothetical other organization and do a culture assessment vis-à-vis that organization. Then, when reality hits, at least you know your own culture to some degree.

Once the new organization is about to be formed, if cultural understanding is to arise it is essential to create dialogue groups to explore each other's shared assumptions. Only by creating reflective dialogues is there a chance to overcome inevitable defensiveness and the illusion of similarity.

After joint operations begin, a new culture is gradually built as the resulting organization together faces new tasks and learns how to deal with them. To speed up cultural learning, you should create such joint tasks early in the life of the new group.

Chapter Nine

Cultural Realities for the Serious Culture Leader

- Realities About What Culture Is
- Realities About What Culture Covers
- Realities About Deciphering Culture
- Realities About Changing Culture
- Realities About Mergers, Acquisitions, and Joint Ventures
- A Final Thought

If you are serious about managing culture in your organization, the biggest danger you face is that you do not fully appreciate the depth and power of culture.

In some forty years of consulting in this area, I have seen over and over how we look for simplifications. When someone comes along and offers us an easier way to assess and manage culture, we leap at it, only to discover later that we were dealing with surface phenomena not linked to real cultural themes. Culture is deep, extensive, and stable. It cannot be taken lightly. If you do not manage culture, it manages you, and you may not even be aware of the extent to which this is happening.

This chapter attempts to take culture seriously. I do not promise you simplicity or easy interventions; I do not promise that you will be able to create and change culture to your heart's desire. I do promise you a dose of reality, which I hope you take seriously so that whatever culture management program you undertake, you deal with cultural forces realistically. The realities I highlight more or less reflect the chapters in the book, but they abstract them and make them sharper. I choose to state these realities as principles and elaborate the logic behind them where appropriate.

Realities About What Culture Is

Culture is the shared tacit assumptions of a group that it has learned in coping with external tasks and dealing with internal relationships.

Although culture manifests itself in overt behavior, rituals, artifacts, climate, and espoused values, its essence is the shared tacit assumptions. As a responsible leader, you must be aware of these assumptions and manage them, or they will manage you.

Unless your organization is a brand new conglomerate of people from other organizations, it has formed a culture that influences all of your thinking and behavior.

If your organization is a new mix, without prior shared experience, then all the members bring their prior cultural experience to the new situation and seek to impose it on that situation.

The quickest way to create a new culture in such a situation is to give people a compelling, common task so that together they can build a new set of assumptions.

The strength and depth of an organization's culture reflects (1) the strength and clarity of the founder of the organization, (2) the amount and intensity of shared experience that organization members have had together, and (3) the degree of success the organization has had.

Culture is, therefore, the product of social learning. Ways of thinking and behavior that are shared *and that work* become elements of the culture.

You cannot, therefore, "create" a new culture. You can demand or stimulate a new way of working and thinking; you can monitor it to make sure that it is done; but members of the organization do not internalize it and make it part of the new culture unless, over time, it actually works better.

A given organization's culture is "right" so long as the organization succeeds in its primary task. If the organization begins to fail, this implies that elements of the culture have become dysfunctional and must change. But the criterion of a right culture is the pragmatic one of what enables the organization to succeed in its primary task.

As the external and internal conditions of an organization change, so does the functionality, or rightness, of given cultural assumptions change. Culture evolves with the fluid circumstances of the organization.

The essential elements of culture are invisible. They are taken for granted and have dropped out of awareness. But they can be brought back into awareness.

Failure to understand culture and take it seriously can have disastrous consequences for an organization.

Superficial understanding of culture can be as dangerous as no understanding at all.

Realities About What Culture Covers

Once organizations have a culture, the shared tacit assumptions that make up the culture influence *all* aspects of organizational functioning. Mission; strategy; means used; measurement systems; correction systems; language; group norms of inclusion and exclusion; status and reward systems; and concepts of time, space, work, and human nature are all reflected in the culture. Culture influences tasks and structure. It cannot be separated as an independent element.

It is especially important for you to understand that mission, strategy, and structure are all colored by cultural assumptions. If you seek objectivity in these areas, you must find outsiders to work with you to help you identify your own cultural biases.

Realities About Deciphering Culture

You cannot use a survey to assess culture. No survey has enough questions to cover all of the relevant areas. Individual employees do not know how to answer many of the questions. Even if they do provide data, you do not know what the salient elements of the culture are relative to some problem you might be trying to solve.

Culture is a group phenomenon. It is shared tacit assumptions. Therefore, the best way to assess it is to bring groups together, to talk about their organization in a structured way that leads them to tacit assumptions.

You can decipher your own cultural biases if you make yourself partially marginal in your own culture. "Travel" to other organizations (cultures) and work with consultants or colleagues from other organizations to reflect on your own tacit, taken-for-granted assumptions.

Realities About the Mechanisms of Transformative Change

Any culture change is transformative because you have to unlearn something before you can learn something new. It is the unlearning that is painful and causes resistance to change.

The motivation to unlearn and learn something new comes from the realization that if you continue in the present way you will not achieve your goals; you will experience "survival anxiety."

But the realization of what may be involved in learning something new causes "learning anxiety" because you may become temporarily incompetent and lose your membership in your group if you learn something new.

For change to occur, survival anxiety must be greater than learning anxiety. This is best achieved by lowering learning anxiety through creating psychological safety for the learner.

If you are the agent of change, the key to managing transformative change is to balance survival anxiety with enough psychological safety to overcome resistance to change.

Realities About Changing Culture

Culture evolves and changes through several different mechanisms which you can influence to varying degrees:

1. General evolution through adaptation to the environment
2. Specific evolution of subgroups to their different environments
3. Guided evolution resulting from cultural "insights" on the part of leaders
4. Guided evolution through empowering selected hybrids from subcultures that are better adapted to current realities
5. Planned and managed culture change through creation of parallel systems of steering committees and project-oriented task forces
6. Partial or total cultural destruction through new leadership that eliminates the carriers of the former culture (turnarounds, bankruptcies, etc.)

Never start with the idea of changing culture. Always start with the issues the organization faces; only when those business issues are clear should you ask yourself whether the culture aids or hinders resolving the issues.

Always think initially of the culture as your source of strength. It is the residue of your past successes. Even if some elements of the culture look dysfunctional, remember that they are probably only a few among a large set of others that continue to be strengths.

If changes need to be made in how the organization is run, try to build on existing cultural strengths rather than attempting to change those elements that may be weaknesses.

If you are in a young and growing organization, you can help to evolve and consolidate the culture, and you can help members get insight into the culture.

If you have time, you can evolve the culture by looking for leaders in the various subcultures that have arisen, locating ones who represent the kind of assumptions you feel are needed in the future, and promoting them into positions of power.

If, in a growing organization, elements of the culture become dysfunctional, you will have a hard time changing them because the culture is so central to the identity of the organization. You may have to replace some of the key leaders and other culture carriers, which can be a very painful process.

If you are in a midlife organization that has clearly dysfunctional elements in its culture, launch a managed change program by creating a parallel system to assess the culture, identify a change program, and implement it.

If you are in a midlife or aging organization that does not have time for a managed change program, you may need to function as a turnaround manager, assess the culture to identify the dysfunctional elements, locate the carriers of those cultural elements, and replace them. This is a painful process.

Realities About Mergers, Acquisitions, and Joint Ventures

Before engaging in any kind of intercultural event, try to get a good sense of your own culture. Train yourself in being culturally sensitive by visiting other organizations and figuring out how their assumptions differ from yours.

If you have the initiative in a merger, acquisition, or joint venture, try to visit the other organization and experience, as much as you can, how things are done there.

Create dialogue groups across any cultural boundary that becomes apparent to you. Do not expect goodwill and experience to produce mutual understanding. Both cultural units need to learn to be reflective to get in touch with their own and each other's assumptions; this can only be done with the dialogue format.

A Final Thought

Learning about culture requires effort. You have to enlarge your perception. You have to examine your own thought process. You have to accept that there are other ways to think and do things.

But once you have acquired what I would call a "cultural perspective," you will be amazed at how rewarding it is. Suddenly the world is much clearer. Anomalies are now explainable, conflicts are more understandable, resistance to change begins to look normal, and—most important—your own humility increases. In that humility, you will find wisdom.

References

Barrett, F. J., and Cooperrider, D. L. "Generative Metaphor Intervention: A New Approach for Working with Systems Divided by Conflict and Caught in Defensive Perception." *Journal of Applied Behavioral Science*, 1990, 26(2), 219–239.

Beckhard, R., and Harris, R. T. *Organizational Transitions: Managing Complex Change*. (2nd ed.). Reading, Mass.: Addison-Wesley, 1987.

Bennis, W. G., and Nanus, B. *Leadership*. New York: HarperCollins, 1985.

Buono, A. F., and Bowditch, J. L. *The Human Side of Mergers and Acquisitions*. San Francisco: Jossey-Bass, 1989.

Bushe, G. R., and Shani, A. B. *Parallel Learning Structures*. Reading, Mass.: Addison-Wesley, 1991.

Cameron, K. S., and Quinn, R. E. *Diagnosing and Changing Organizational Culture*. Reading, Mass.: Addison-Wesley, 1999.

Centre for Organization Studies. *Mergers and Acquisitions*. Working Document No. 1. Barcelona: Centre for Organization Studies, 1990.

Collins, J. C., and Porras, J. I. *Built to Last*. New York: HarperBusiness, 1994.

Donaldson, G., and Lorsch, J. W. *Decision Making at the Top*. New York: Basic Books, 1983.

Dyer, W. G., Jr. *Culture Change in Family Firms*. San Francisco: Jossey-Bass, 1986.

Goffee, R., and Jones, G. *The Character of a Corporation*. New York: HarperCollins, 1998.

Hall, E. T. *The Silent Language*. New York: Doubleday, 1959.

Hall, E. T. *The Hidden Dimension*. New York: Doubleday, 1966.

Hofstede, G. *Culture's Consequences*. Thousand Oaks, Calif.: Sage, 1980.

Hofstede, G. *Cultures and Organizations*. London: McGraw-Hill, 1991.

Isaacs, W. *Dialogue and the Art of Thinking Together*. New York: Doubleday, 1999.

Isaacs, W. N. "Taking Flight: Dialogue, Collective Thinking, and Organizational Learning." *Organizational Dynamics*, Winter 1993, 24–39.

Kluckhohn, F. R., and Strodtbeck, F. L. *Variations in Value Orientations*. New York: HarperCollins, 1961.

Kotter, J. P., and Heskett, J. L. *Corporate Culture and Performance*. New York: Free Press, 1992.

Kouzes, J. M., and Posner, B. Z. *The Leadership Challenge*. San Francisco: Jossey-Bass, 1995.

McGregor, D. *The Human Side of Enterprise*. New York: McGraw-Hill, 1960.

McManus, M. L., and Hergert, M. L. *Surviving Merger and Acquisition*. Glenview, Ill.: Scott, Foresman, 1988.

Roth, G. "In Search of the Paperless Office: The Structuring Waves of Technological Change." Unpublished Ph.D. dissertation, MIT Sloan School of Management, 1993.

Salk, J. E. "International Shared Management Joint Venture Teams." Unpublished Ph.D. dissertation, MIT Sloan School of Management, 1992.

Schein, E. H. *Organizational Culture and Leadership*. (1st ed.). San Francisco: Jossey-Bass, 1985.

Schein, E. H. *Process Consultation: Lessons for Managers and Consultants*. Reading, Mass.: Addison-Wesley, 1987.

Schein, E. H. *Organizational Culture and Leadership*. (2nd ed.). San Francisco: Jossey-Bass, 1992.

Schein, E. H. "On Dialogue, Culture, and Organizational Learning." *Organizational Dynamics*, Autumn 1993, *22*, 40–51.

Schein, E. H. "Three Cultures of Management: The Key to Organizational Learning. *Sloan Management Review*, 1996, *38*(1), 9–20.

Schein, E. H. *Process Consultation Revisited*. Reading, Mass.: Addison-Wesley, 1999.

Thomas, R. *What Machines Can't Do*. Berkeley: University of California Press, 1994.

Tichy, N. M., and Devanna, M. A. *The Transformational Leader*. New York: Wiley, 1986.

Van Maanen, J., and Barley, S. R. "Occupational Communities: Culture and Control in Organizations." In B. M. Staw and L. L. Cummings (eds.), *Research in Organizational Behavior, Vol. 6*. Greenwich, Conn.: JAI Press, 1984.

Zand, D. E. "Collateral Organization: A New Change Strategy." *Journal of Applied Behavioral Science*, 1974, *10*, 63–89.

Index

S

T

U

V

W

Z